FAMILIES

Shelley Day Sclater

Series Editor: Paul Selfe

DEDICATION

To the memory of my mother and my father, Gwen and George Day

Orders: please contact Bookpoint Ltd, 39 Milton Park, Abingdon, Oxon OX14 4TD.
Telephone: (44) 01235 400414, Fax: (44) 01235 400454. Lines are open from 9.00–6.00,
Monday to Saturday, with a 24 hour message answering service.
Email address: orders@bookpoint.co.uk

A catalogue record for this title is available from The British Library

ISBN 0 340 75832 5

First published 2000
Impression number 10 9 8 7 6 5 4 3 2 1
Year   2005 2004 2003 2002 2001 2000

Cover photo from the Tate Gallery: 'Family Group Earth Red and Yellow' 1953
Dame Barbara Hepworth, copyright © Alan Bowness, Hepworth Estate.

Typeset by Transet Limited, Coventry, England.
Printed in Great Britain for Hodder & Stoughton Educational, a division of
Hodder Headline plc, 338 Euston Road, London NW1 3BH by Redwood Books,
Trowbridge, Wilts.

CONTENTS

ACKNOWLEDGEMENTS

Thanks first to my students on the Family Studies course at the University of East London, and to those on the Social and Political Sciences Tripos at Cambridge, with whom I have rehearsed the material in this book over the years. Thanks also to colleagues who have assisted by reading drafts, making suggestions, providing information or clarifying points, in particular; Andrew Bainham, Carol Compton, Gill Dunne, John Hardisty, Ginny Morrow and Bethan Rees. As always, I am grateful to Stephanie Macek, Librarian at the Social and Political Sciences Faculty, Cambridge, for assisting with access to bibliographic material. Staff in the Official Publications Room at Cambridge University Library also helped with locating statistical material. Thanks to my daughter, Poppy, an A level student herself, for reading parts of the text and providing me with assurance that it was comprehensible. Many others have contributed to this book, through what they have said and what they have written, which has helped to shape my thinking; I am endebted to them. I would like also to thank Margaret O'Brien, who has always encouraged my interest in Family Studies, and Martin Richards who gave me the first opportunity to teach. Paul Selfe, the series editor, was extremely helpful in making suggestions to improve the text and I would like to thank the editors at Hodder & Stoughton, Luke Hacker and Emma Knights, for their careful work. Thanks to all of you who helped, wittingly or unwittingly. The responsibility for interpretations, errors and omissions, however, remains my own.

The publishers would like to thank:
The Women's Aid Federation of England for permission to reproduce the poster on p.102.
The Office for National Statistics © Crown Copyright 1999 for permission to use material from their Marriage and Divorce Statistics on p.73.
PA News photo library for permission to reproduce the photographs on p.92 and p.108.
Laura Salisbury/GAZE International for permission to reproduce the photograph on p.10.
The Tate Gallery/Alan Bowness © (Hepworth Estate) for permission to reproduce the cover painting: 'Family Group Earth Red and Yellow' 1953.
Denis Paquin and Associated Press for permission to reproduce the photograph on p.53.

1

INTRODUCTION

HOW TO USE THE BOOK

EACH CHAPTER IN this book examines one or more of the central debates relating to the sociology of families. The text is devised for readers with little or no background knowledge in the subject, and there are Study Points and Activities throughout to encourage a consideration of the issues raised. Student readers are advised to make use of these and answer them either on paper or in group discussion, a particularly fruitful way of learning; they will assist them to develop the skills of interpretation, analysis and evaluation. There are many ways of preparing for an exam, but a thorough understanding of the material is obviously crucial.

Each chapter is structured to give a clear understanding of the authors, concepts and issues that you need to know about. To assist understanding and facilitate later revision, it is often helpful to make concise notes.

MAKING NOTES FROM THE BOOK

Linear notes
- Bold headings establish key points: names, theories and concepts.
- Subheadings indicate details of relevant issues.
- A few numbered points list related arguments.

Diagram or pattern notes
- Use a large blank sheet of paper and write a key idea in the centre.
- Make links between this and related issues.
- Show also the connections between sub issues which share features in common.

Both systems have their advantages and disadvantages, and may take some time to perfect. Linear notes can be little more than a copy of what is already in the book and patterned notes can be confusing. But if you practise the skill, they can reduce material efficiently and concisely becoming invaluable for revision. Diagrammatic notes may be very useful for those with a strong visual memory and provide a clear overview of a whole issue, showing patterns of interconnection. The introduction of helpful drawings or a touch of humour into the format is often a good way to facilitate the recall of names, research studies and complex concepts.

Activity
Make a diagram to show the two ways of making notes with their possible advantages and disadvantages

SKILLS ADVICE

Students must develop and display certain skills for their examination and recognise which ones are being tested in a question. The clues are frequently in key words in the opening part. The skill domains are:

1 **Knowledge and understanding:** the ability to discuss the views of the main theorists; their similarities and differences; the strengths and weaknesses of evidence. To gain marks students must display this when asked to *explain, examine, suggest a method, outline reasons*.
2 **Interpretation, application and analysis:** the use of evidence in a logical, relevant way, either to show how it supports arguments or refutes them. Students must show this ability when asked *identify, use items A/B/C, draw conclusions from a table*.
3 **Evaluation:** the skill of assessing evidence in a balanced way so that logical conclusions follow. Students can recognise this skill when asked to *assess, critically examine, comment on levels of reliability, compare and contrast*, or if asked to *what extent*.

Activity
Draw an evaluation table, as below, using the whole of an A4 page. Examine studies as you proceed in your work and fill in the relevant details. Keep it for revision purposes.

Sociologist		
Title of the study	Strengths	Weaknesses
Verdict		
Judgement/justification		

REVISION ADVICE

- Keep clear notes at all times in a file or on disk (with back up copy).
- Be familiar with exam papers and their demands.
- Become familiar with key authors, their theories, their research and sociological concepts.

Activity

Make and keep **Key Concept Cards**, as shown below.

COLLECTIVE CONSCIENCE

Key idea

A term used by **Durkheim** meaning:

- The existence of a social and moral order exterior to individuals and acting upon them as an independent force.
- The shared sentiments, beliefs and values of individuals which make up the **collective conscience.**
- In **traditional societies** it forms the basis of social order.
- As societies modernise the collective conscience weakens: **mechanical solidarity** is replaced by **organic solidarity**.

Key theorist: Emile Durkheim

Syllabus area: Functionalism

EXAMINATION ADVICE

To develop an effective method of writing, answers should be:

- **Sociological:** use the language and research findings of sociologists; do not use anecdotal opinion gathered from people not involved in sociology to support arguments.

- **Adequate in length:** enough is written to obtain the marks available.
- **Interconnected** with other parts of the syllabus (such as stratification, gender, ethnicity).
- **Logical:** the answer follows from the relevant evidence.
- **Balanced:** arguments and counter arguments are weighed; references are suitable.
- **Accurate:** reliable data is obtained from many sources.

The three skill areas on p 2 should be demonstrated, so that the question is answered effectively.

In displaying knowledge, the student is not necessarily also demonstrating interpretation.

- This must be specified with phrases like 'Therefore, this study leads to the view that...'
- Sections of answers should hang together, one leading to the next. This shows how the question is being answered by a process of analysis based on the evidence.
- Reach a conclusion based on the evidence used and the interpretations made.

The skill of evaluation is often regarded (not necessarily accurately) as the most problematic. Evaluation means being judge and jury; the strengths and weaknesses of evidence is assessed and an overall judgement about its value is made. To evaluate an argument or theory, consider whether it usefully opens up debate; explains the events studied; does it have major weaknesses?

Activity

Look through some past examination papers and pick out the evaluation questions. Underline the evaluation words and work out which skills are required.

COURSEWORK ADVICE

Coursework provides an opportunity to carry out a study using primary and/or secondary data to investigate an issue of sociological interest, and must address theoretical issues. The suggestions included at the end of each chapter may be adapted or used to generate further ideas. Final decision must be agreed with a teacher or tutor.

MAKING A PLAN

Before starting a piece of coursework, you should make a plan:

1 Read and make notes from articles describing research projects in journals.
2 Have a clear aim in mind; choose an issue that interests you and is within your ability.
3 Decide more precisely what you want to know; establish a simple hypothesis to test.
4 Select a range of possible methods; consider both quantitative and qualitative.
5 Decide on a range of possible sources of information.
6 List the people to whom you can seek help, perhaps including a statistician.

WRITING THE PROJECT

1 Seek frequent advice from a teacher or tutor.
2 Check the weighting for different objectives in the marking scheme.
3 Keep clear notes throughout, including new ideas and any problems that arise.
4 Limit its length (maximum 5,000 words).
5 Label and index the study in the following way:
   a **Rationale:** a reason for choosing the subject; preliminary observations on the chosen area
   b **Context:** an outline of the theoretical and empirical context of the study
   c **Methodology:** a statement of the methodology used and reasons for selecting it
   d **Content:** presentation of the evidence and/or argument including results
   e **Evaluation:** the outcomes are weighed and strengths and weaknesses noted.
   f **Sources:** all the sources of information are listed.
OR
   a **Title**
   b **Contents**
   c **Abstract:** a brief summary of the aims, methods, findings and evaluation.
   d **Rationale**
   e **The Study**
   f **Research Diary**
   g **Bibliography**
   h **Appendix:** to include proposal for the study, single examples of a questionnaire or other data-gathering instrument and transcripts of interviews.
   i **Annex:** to include raw data gathered.

Paul Selfe
Series editor

2

WHAT IS 'THE FAMILY'?

Introduction

WHAT IS 'THE family'? Nothing is more commonplace in our society than the concept of 'family'. It is something that we all know about and will have some direct experience of. From the earliest days of our lives our ideas about family derive from this experience and from what we see around us. Importantly, we are also surrounded by media representations of family; in stories and newspaper reports, in magazines, on TV, in books, advertisements and films we can identify the many images of family which pervade our culture. In their speeches, politicians of all persuasions frequently invoke ideas about *the* family, and remind us of the fundamental importance of *family values*.

Yet, sociology tells us that family is a complex concept. Sociologists say that there is no such thing as *the* family, no single definition that can encompass the myriad of domestic and kinship arrangements that characterise contemporary social life. Broad agreement on family values, too, would be difficult to identify across society as a whole. Sociologists point to, for example, the diversity of family patterns in different ethnic groups within a society, and in different social classes at different historical periods. Despite its familiarity, sociologists agree that family is an elusive concept that defies any universal definition. For this reason, contemporary sociologists prefer to talk about *families* rather than about *the* family.

This chapter discusses the range of meanings of 'the family', and highlights the difficulties in arriving at a single definition that can encompass the variety of family forms in contemporary society. If we look around us, we can see a whole range of different domestic arrangements that count as 'family'. 'Family' means different things to different people.

Table 1: *Key concepts and issues in this chapter*	
KEY CONCEPTS	KEY ISSUES
Family	What is 'the family'?
Family values	How are families changing?
Nuclear family	What kinds of images of families are there in our culture?
Extended family	
Kinship	Is the family in decline?
Household	
Marriage	
Cohabitation	
Monogamy	
Intimacy	
Family ideology	

KEY CONCEPTS AND THEIR DEFINITIONS

Trying to provide definitions for important sociological concepts can be a useful way of organising information. The following list provides some definitions for some of the significant concepts in family sociology. Note that these definitions can only be widely agreed upon because they are broad and rather vague:

Family: a group of people related to one another by 'blood', marriage or adoption. Members of families often share accommodation.

Nuclear Family: this consists of parents and their dependent children (two generations).

Extended Family: this is the addition of wider kin to the nuclear family. Such kin can include a third generation (grandparents), or the brothers and sisters of adult members (uncles and aunts) or other members of the families of such wider kin.

Kinship: this refers to the larger family group where relationships are based on 'blood' (genetics) or marriage. In most cultures, kinship defines the basis of the rights and responsibilities family members have in relation to each other. Ideas about kinship often inform the law (for example, the law of inheritance and succession).

Household: a group of people, who may or may not be related to each other, who share living accommodation.

'THE FAMILY' OR 'FAMILIES'?

Sociologists have always been interested in families, and in the role that families play in society. Some early sociologists thought that families were universal, and that they existed in all societies in all historical periods. But evidence from anthropology and from history cast doubt upon that assumption. Research by anthropologists working in different cultures, and research by historians on previous historical periods, showed that families were very much a product of place and time. In the 1950s, sociologists of the *Functionalist School* saw families as *social institutions* that were intrinsically linked to other social institutions and structures (such as the economy) and they saw families as serving particular functions in society. The ideas about the family that derived from *Functionalism* are discussed further in chapter 3.

In our own society, family patterns have undergone rapid change in the last 50 years. Britain is a multi–cultural society, and a range of family patterns characterise different cultural groups. For example, in the Afro–Caribbean community, lone–mother families are almost as common as two–parent families, whereas in Asian communities, lone–mother families are only a small minority, and families consisting of people from several different generations are much more common. Sociologists now recognise that families exist in a multitude of different forms and, for this reason, they tend to talk about 'families' rather than 'the family', as the latter term tends to imply that there is only one legitimate family form.

Study point

On the basis of your own experience, write down what the term 'family' means to you. Compare your ideas with other students in your group. What are the main points that emerge?

FAMILIES AND SOCIETY

In their studies of families, sociologists are interested in the connection between social structures and individual lives. Families are important *social institutions* but they are also about *intimate relationships*; families have great personal and emotional significance for most people. As social institutions, families perform particular *functions* in society, for example, the *socialisation* of children. They also define the *roles* to be played by particular family members, for example, mother, father, wife, husband. Traditionally, these roles have been based on gender and age. Roles are not just about who does what in the family, but they are also about who has power and about how obligations are shared out. Nowadays, family roles are more a matter for negotiation than they once were; they are less fixed. For example, some fathers carry out caring and nurturing activities that were previously the province of women. These changes in family relationships reflect broader social and cultural change in society as a whole. In this way, families are intimately linked to society and culture and at the same time they reflect the changing aspirations and needs of women, men and children.

Study point
Men are just as capable of caring for young children as women, given the opportunity. Do you agree?

IMAGES OF 'THE FAMILY'

There is an image of 'the family' which remains dominant in our society, although it is increasingly being challenged by new ideas that emphasise diversity. This dominant image is what sociologists call the 'nuclear' family. It consists of married parents and their dependent children, living together in one household. In statistical terms, nuclear families comprise only a minority of households, but they still tend to be regarded as *the norm*. Images of such families appear, for example, in advertisements, films and soaps, and they can also be seen to inform social policies. These images appear as ideals (sometimes called the 'cornflake packet' family) that we are implicitly invited to aspire to.

Importantly, the existence of these images means that other family forms, such as lone-parent households, or gay families, appear as *deviant* or undesirable in some way. We can see these ideas reflected often in politicians' speeches and in the ways in which the mass media often blame broader social problems on the 'breakdown' of families. For example, concerns about high levels of youth crime have been attributed to divorce and to the absence of fathers as role models for young men. There is an implicit assumption that the two–parent, nuclear family is best and is what is needed for the optimum development of children, and to guarantee a stable society.

Study point
Make a list of sources (e.g. advertisements, political speeches) where you would expect to find images of families. Examine three of the sources. Can you identify a dominant image or images?

A GAY COUPLE WITH TWO TEENAGE CHILDREN FROM PREVIOUS MARRIAGES – OFTEN CONSIDERED A DEVIANT FAMILY FORM.

Today, sociologists do not accept such images as accurately portraying the truth of the matter. On the contrary, they argue that such images indicate the ways in which 'the family' is socially constructed according to prevailing *ideologies*. The ideology of the family is a powerful one, and it is one in which we all make some emotional investment. Families carry a profound emotional significance for all of us. When things go wrong, either in our own family, or when 'the family' seems to be threatened at a social level (for example, as indicated by a high divorce rate), it is understandable that we experience some degree of disorientation and anxiety. In recent years, social changes in family structures and patterns have given rise to such anxieties, leading some to argue that there is a contemporary 'crisis in the family' that threatens social stability and cohesion.

CHANGING FAMILIES

Governments routinely collect statistical data about family structures and patterns. This is publicly available in publications from the *Office for National Statistics* and journals such as *Social Trends* and *Population Trends*. These data indicate that family structures and household patterns are changing, and that there has been particularly dramatic social change in this area since the 1950s. These demographic changes have given rise to intense debates about what is happening to families and family values in Britain today.

Activity
Consult issues of *Social Trends* or *Population Trends* to find out about the changes that have occurred in marriage and divorce rates since 1961.

THE DECLINE OF THE FAMILY?

There can be no doubt that family life is changing. This is so in all Western European countries, as well as in the United States. Some sociologists have regarded these changes as evidence that there is a 'decline in the family' or a 'demise of family values'. Others, by contrast, take the view that 'the family' is fluid and has always been the subject of historical change. Yet others have emphasised the persistence of continuities alongside the changes, and have been at pains to point out the multi–dimensional nature of family life, and to stress the fact that changes in one dimension are not necessarily accompanied by changes in others. Thus, a debate has arisen concerning both the meanings and the impact of contemporary social changes in family structures and patterns.

Study point
Suggest at least five reasons why some commentators say that the family is in decline.

DEMOGRAPHIC TRENDS

Evidence from demographic sources, such as is routinely collected by the government, indicates trends that show the changing nature of families over the last thirty years or so. More people marry later, marriage is becoming less popular and more people are getting divorced than in the 1960s. More people are cohabiting, whether as a prelude to, or as a substitute for, marriage. More women are bringing up children on their own, either due to divorce, or as a result of relationship breakdown. Women are having fewer children and are starting their families later. Births outside marriage are increasing all the time, although about half are jointly registered in both parents' names and the majority of children continue to live with both natural parents. More women are choosing not to have children at all. The proportion of older people (over 65) in the population, many of them living alone, has increased and seems likely to increase further. More married women go out to work; most fathers continue to work full–time, whilst mothers continue to do most of the unpaid work in the home. These are the undisputed general trends that we can glean from national statistics. They indicate that profound changes in family arrangements are afoot and at the same time they remind us that we must not ignore the many continuities.

Study point
How might you account for the declining popularity of marriage?

The changes that have occurred in family structures and patterns over the last 50 years may be summarised as follows:

- People tend to marry at a later age than they did before (the median age for marriage is now the mid–20s)
- The marriage rate has declined
- The divorce rate has risen
- Cohabitation is becoming more popular (whether as a prelude to, or as a substitute for, marriage)
- The remarriage rate amongst divorced people has fallen
- More women (and some men) are bringing up children on their own (whether as a matter of choice or as a result of relationship breakdown)
- Women are having fewer children and are having them later in life
- More women are choosing to remain childless
- Births outside marriage are increasing (although many such births are jointly registered by cohabiting parents)
- A rising proportion of the population is elderly (and increasing numbers of aged people live alone)
- More married women are going out to work.

SOCIAL ATTITUDES

Whilst we must recognise the many changes in demographic patterns, we should also not ignore the continuities that persist. These are, perhaps, most marked in relation to social attitudes. Every year, a *Social Attitudes Survey* is carried out. This usually, but not always, includes some information and data about attitudes towards family life. These opinion surveys suggest that there is a gap between the demographic data about what is actually happening to families and what people think ought to be happening. In other words, there is a gap between what people say they believe and what they actually do.

The demographic data have indicated profound social changes in relation to family structures and patterns. But the attitudes data indicate a remarkable persistence of 'traditional' values in relation to families, although there is some indication of changing attitudes amongst younger people, suggesting that if they maintain their more progressive attitudes, the gap may well be set to decrease over time. For example, a substantial proportion of people think that divorce should be made more difficult, and the majority agree that, to grow up happily, children need a home in which both father and mother are present. Most continue to believe that mothers of young children should be at home with them. Interestingly, most also believe that men ought to play a greater role in child care. The sociological evidence suggests that fathers continue to play only a peripheral role, even where both parents are working full–time.

Activities

List the main ways in which family patterns have changed in recent years according to (a) the demographic evidence and (b) evidence on social attitudes. How might you account for the difference between (a) and (b)?

Make a list of the social changes that you think might have an influence on the divorce rate. Compare your ideas with other students. Decide which changes you think are most significant.

Sociologists have predicted that these general trends will continue. They argue that, in future, more people will never marry; most couples will cohabit instead, and a greater proportion of children will be born to cohabiting couples. At least one third, and possibly nearer one half, of marriages will end in divorce and fewer people will remarry. An increasing number of children will live in lone-parent families or with a step–parent.

The main findings from recent data about social attitudes regarding family life may be summarised as follows:

- Cohabitation, as a *substitute* for marriage, does not have popular support
- Cohabitation as a *prelude* to marriage, or as a stage in courtship, attracts popular support
- Monogamy (one partner at a time) and fidelity (faithfulness to that partner) are widely held values

- Most people think that people who want to have children ought to get married
- Only a small proportion of people think that personal freedom is more important than the companionship of marriage
- Opinion is about equally divided on whether or not a working mother has just as warm and secure a relationship with her children as a mother who does not work outside the home
- Most people no longer think that children will suffer if their mothers go out to work, but most also think that family life is happier when mothers do not go out to work
- Less than half of people agree that a single parent can bring up a child as well as a married couple
- Only a small percentage agree that gay men and lesbians should have the right to marry

Activity

Undertake a short study to find the attitudes of a group with regard to the future roles of men and women in the family.

FAMILY CHANGE: A MATTER OF DEBATE

Whether these changes are evidence of a 'decline in the family' or whether they represent a continuation of historical change in family structures and patterns, is a matter of some debate in sociology that cannot be decided on the basis of evidence alone. Certainly, families have always been subject to change. It has been common throughout history for children to experience diverse forms of family life and to be looked after by persons other than their natural parents. For example, in the days before divorce was common, children would often lose a parent by death. Family and community life, and the ways in which they change over time, are highly complex (the historical evidence is discussed in chapter 4). It is not possible to decide, on the basis of the evidence, that the changes we are witnessing are peculiar to our own age.

Points of Evaluation

1 It helps to recognise that family life is *multi–dimensional*.
2 Family life consists of practices (what people actually are doing, as reflected in the demographic evidence), and values (what people say they believe, as reflected in the evidence about attitudes).
3 Family life also involves ideologies (the ideas about and images of families that pervade popular culture and political rhetoric).

4 As we have seen, some of these dimensions can be at odds with others, at the same time.

5 Changes in one dimension are not necessarily accompanied by parallel changes in another.

For example, take the case of teenage pregnancy, an issue that has provoked the concern of governments from time to time. The prevailing view is that teenage girls who fall pregnant are either acting irresponsibly or are lacking sex education and information. The implication in this view is that pregnancy is an avoidable accident. An alternative view is that young women who give birth are lacking neither responsibility nor information, but rather that they have made a personal choice to have a baby in order to facilitate the difficult transition to independent adulthood status by becoming parents and establishing a family of their own. The *ideology of the family* is so powerful that we should not imagine that teenage girls should be exempt from its influence.

THE FAMILY: A MATTER OF CHOICE?

One thing that may be peculiar to our age is the issue of personal choice. However, this needs to be seen in the context of the diversity of family forms. As we shall discuss in chapter 5, in some sections of society, the issue of choice is an important one; for example, gay men and lesbian women are actively choosing families that depart, quite radically, from the nuclear ideal. On the other hand, individual choices are necessarily constrained by the prevailing values of a given cultural group. Some British Asian families, for example, have opted to continue traditional practices of arranging marriages and many give priority to sustaining broader kin networks, despite the trend, in Britain as a whole, towards individual choice in family matters. Overall, sociologists see people as less bound today by ideas of duty and responsibility in relation to the family than they were forty or fifty years ago. For example, Janet Finch shows how caring for older people in the family context has become less a matter of accepted duty and more a matter of individual choice; we no longer feel as bound by the same notions of family responsibility as our grandparents might have been.

MEANINGS OF 'FAMILY'

Linked to this are changing meanings of the term 'family'. Some sociologists argue that 'family' is no longer a structural entity, but has become a 'relational' one. The meaning of 'family' as a social institution has changed. Its structural and functional importance to society is being challenged by its transformation into a more relational concept, as the personal relationships within families assume greater significance. This transition is reflected, for example, in the accounts that children give of concepts of 'family'. Sociologists have found, in work with children, that children's definitions of 'family' are based on relational and emotional ties, and not on 'blood' ties or ideas about structure or social function.

LOVE AND INTIMACY

Other sociologists have identified changes in the perception of intimacy, which help to explain why marriage is becoming less popular and divorce more common, whilst cohabitation is on the increase. Sociologist Anthony Giddens argues that the 'romantic' search for the perfect partner, for Mr or Mrs 'Right', has been replaced in contemporary society by the search for the perfect relationship. He argues that, where one relationship fails to satisfy, the contemporary individual is no longer bound by ideas of duty, 'for richer, for poorer, in sickness and in health, till death us do part', but rather is more influenced by ideas of self–fulfilment and self–actualisation. This self–actualising individual feels free to move on to try to find a more satisfying and fulfilling relationship. Thus, according to Giddens, patterns of intimacy have changed and, with them, the meanings of intimacy and marriage. 'Love', in contemporary society, is no longer romantic, but pragmatic and contingent; it no longer has a 'forever–after' quality, but will be abandoned if it fails to satisfy.

Study point
Explain the idea that love is no longer romantic but pragmatic and contingent. Do you agree?

In this way, sociologists have accounted for the ways in which marriage is being increasingly replaced by what they call 'serial monogamy', as people pursue successive relationships in search of the 'right' one that can satisfy their own needs for self–fulfilment. Thus, the incidence of marriage has declined, and that of cohabitation has increased. A linked development is the increasing separation that we are witnessing between marriage and reproduction and parenthood. Marriage, as a basis for the bearing and rearing of children, is on the decline, as more people are separating and divorcing and an increasing number of children are born to unmarried couples (many register the baby jointly and are living together at the same address) and lone mothers.

In this context, we can see that the question of 'what is the family?' permits no easy or straightforward answers. Families are historically and culturally specific, and the meaning of the term is apt to shift depending upon our vantage point. Families change as society changes, and perhaps this has always been the case. But social change is not uniform; some aspects or dimensions of change outstrip, or even contradict, others. We have seen, for example, that there is currently a gap between the evidence we can glean from demographic statistics and that which reveals itself in surveys of social attitudes. It is necessary, however, to tolerate this kind of uncertainty and ambiguity if we are to learn to be good sociologists.

SUMMARY

'Family' is a familiar term, but it is difficult to arrive at a precise definition with which everyone agrees. We all have some experience of families, and images of families reach us all the time through the media. The dominant image tends to be that of the nuclear family but, in reality, people organise their domestic lives in a range of different ways, and an increasing number of people are choosing not to follow 'traditional' routes. Sociologists today, therefore, tend to avoid talking about *the* family and instead acknowledge difference and diversity by talking about *families*.

The family is both a *social institution* and a *set of personal relationships*. Families stand between individuals and their society, performing social functions (such as the socialisation of children) that benefit society, and providing a place for intimacy, emotional experience and personal security. Sociologists recognise, however, that families are not always 'havens', but can be *dysfunctional*, and the locus for problems such as domestic violence and child abuse.

Over the last 50 years or so, family forms and patterns have undergone rapid social change. Some, especially those on the right wing of politics, have interpreted the effect of these changes to mean that the family is losing its functions, which are increasingly being taken over by the State. Others disagree, and point instead to the changing functions of the family, and how these are becoming more specialised and supported by the State.

There has also been a debate about the future of the family. Some sociologists see the changes in family forms and patterns as threatening the future of the family; they see the family as 'in decline', which raises questions about the long term effects of such changes on society as a whole. Others see the family as merely changing, not declining, and point out that families have always changed in accordance with socio–historical and economic circumstances; they say that there is no cause for alarm.

There is some discrepancy between these changes as they are manifested in demographic statistics, and how they appear in data about social attitudes. The former tend to emphasise quite dramatic social change (such as in falling marriage rates, increasing divorce rates, and increasing numbers of children born outside of marriage). The latter, by contrast, tend to show the remarkable persistence of many traditional attitudes towards family life. Thus, there is a gap between what people seem to be doing in families, and the values they say they believe in.

STUDY GUIDES

Group activities

1 Make a list of at least 15 keywords or ideas that you associate with 'family'. Complete the following sentence in less than 20 words: 'Families are ...' Compare your definition with other students and discuss the similarities and differences between them. Can you arrive at a definition with which everyone in the group agrees?

2 Devise a list of questions designed to help you ascertain which 'family values' people think are important, and why. Use the questions to conduct some research in your class.

3 You should have access to journals such as *Social Trends* and *Population Trends* which gives information about social developments on the basis of statistics collected routinely by the government. In your group, consult the appropriate issues to find out how marriage, cohabitation and divorce rates have changed since the Second World War. Collate your findings into a table.

Practice questions

Item A

For more than a century and a half, a particular model of family life has been dominant. It is, essentially, the model of the middle–class Victorian family: the private, self–contained unit, with breadwinning father married to non–employed caring mother and two or more children. It has never been universal. However, it has exerted a forceful influence as an *ideal*. The origins of its influence can be traced to Victorian philanthropy: in the interests of reforming the working classes and saving them from the iniquities forced upon them by industrialisation, the well–meaning middle classes set about teaching temperance and respectability — a package including a system of values about family life which emphasised maternal care, domesticity and privacy. Gradually, over many decades, the middle–class model spread into working class communities. By the 1950s, it had become conventional for a working–class woman to be isolated at home, with her children as her prime concern and the centre of her attention, while her husband went out to earn a living for them all. The family was seen as a refuge, a 'haven in a heartless world'.

Coote, Harman and Hewitt (1994) 'Changing Family Structures and Family Behaviour', in Eekelaar and Maclean (eds) *A Reader on Family Law*, Oxford University Press, p43.

Item B

Dominant family patterns also change as a result of changes in other spheres of activity. As Medick (1976) has expressed it, families and households can only be understood properly when they are seen as component elements of wider systems of production, consumption and reproduction. Yet how families produce, consume and reproduce, what part they play within these processes, will inevitably depend on the modes of production, consumption and reproduction in the society, or more accurately dominant within that part of the social and economic formation occupied by that individual family unit. Thus, for example, the demands made on families involved in peasant/subsistence farming differ from those made on families during early phases of industrialisation and urban growth, and equally are different to those developing in late modernity.

Graham Allen, (1999) *The Sociology of the Family: A Reader*, Blackwell, p3.

1   Suggest four ways in which the dominant ideal of the nuclear family is produced and maintained.
2   With reference to the Items and elsewhere, how would you account for the continuing dominance of the nuclear family ideal in western industrialised cultures?
3   Items A and B both suggest that broader social processes exert an influence on family forms and patterns. Suggest three ways in which individuals and families may, reciprocally, influence the direction of social change.
4   List seven dimensions of demographic change in family forms and patterns since the 1950s.
5   With reference to elsewhere, identify three factors that have contributed to changing family patterns since the 1950s.

Coursework suggestions

1   Write an essay: Is the family in decline, or is it merely changing?
2   Compare and contrast the evidence from (a) demographic sources and (b) social attitudes surveys that indicates the nature of current family patterns and values.
3   Critically evaluate the proposition that the nuclear family is the norm in contemporary British society.

3

FUNCTIONALISM AND ITS CRITICS

Introduction

FUNCTIONALISM WAS A school of thought in sociology that was dominant after the Second World War until at least the 1960s. The school is so named because of the emphasis it places on the *functions* played in society by a range of social *structures* and social *institutions*, including 'the family'. Note that Functionalism is sometimes referred to as *Structural Functionalism*; this highlights the importance placed on the underlying political and economic structures of society for social organisation. Functionalism presented a rosy image of the family, and was associated with what has been called the 'golden age' of the nuclear family after the Second World War. Functionalist theories have been very influential, but they have also been subjected to much criticism. This chapter explains the Functionalist approach to the family and discusses the major strands of critical thought.

The most important points of the Functionalist view of the family may be summarised as follows:

- 'The family' can only be fully understood in the context of the whole *social system* of which it is but one part.
- 'The family' is closely linked to other institutions in the social system.
- 'The family' is functional, both for individual members and for society as a whole. It is the cornerstone of society; it is what guarantees social stability and cohesion.
- The isolated *nuclear* family is the dominant form in industrialised societies; it is this form that best fits with the needs both of individual members and of an industrialised economy.
- The *extended* family is typical of pre–industrialised societies, and no longer has a place in modern industrialised economies.

Table 2: *Key theorists, concepts and issues: Functionalism*		
KEY THEORISTS	KEY CONCEPTS	KEY ISSUES
T. Parsons	Social institutions	Is the family the cornerstone of society?
W.J. Goode	Social system	
G. Murdock	Functional unit	What are the functions of the family?
M. Young and P. Wilmott	Nuclear family	How does the family support the needs of the industrialised economy?
R. Fletcher	Public/private division	How have the functions of the family changed?
	Sex role differentiation	
	The symmetrical family	

TALCOTT PARSONS AND THE FUNCTIONALIST SCHOOL

The most well-known theorist of the Functionalist school was the American sociologist, Talcott Parsons. He argued that the typical family form in industrialised societies, and the one that best 'fit' the needs of the economy, was the *nuclear* family. It was able to perform its functions because of its relative isolation (from the 'public' world of wage labour, and from the extended family), enabling it to be socially and geographically mobile. He saw this family as having two essential functions:

- The *socialisation* of children; the meeting of their developmental needs and the transmission, across generations, of social norms and values.
- The *stabilisation* of the emotions of the adults; the family provided a locus for the contained expression of emotional and sexual needs, that otherwise would be disruptive of society.

In keeping with the dominant orientation in sociology at the time, Parsons' approach was a *scientific* one; he thought that sociology could provide a value–free science of the family, that could be applied to promote the well–being of society and of the individuals within it. In his view, 'the family' occupied a *private sphere*, quite separate from the *public* world of work and the economy. He saw this separation as necessary to enable the family to perform its essential functions in the smooth running of society. The family mediated between individuals and society, meeting the needs of individuals for security, development and personal satisfaction, and the needs of society for reproduction, maintenance and the socialisation of new members of society who would become the labour force of the future. He saw the nuclear family as having evolved to meet the needs of an industrialised economy; it consisted of small, mobile collections of people who were largely free of community and kinship pressures, and who could therefore meet the needs for labour mobility.

Central to the Functionalist account was the idea of *sex–role differentiation*. Men and women performed different tasks within the family, based largely upon assumed biological imperatives. Men, Parsons said, performed an *instrumental* role, that of economic provider (or 'breadwinner') whilst women's role was an *expressive* one, as nurturer and emotional provider. Men were seen as primarily located in the *public* world of work, returning in the evenings to the home, to what Christopher Lasch characterised as 'the haven in a heartless world', where women dominated the *private* sphere, servicing the needs of their employed husbands and their dependent children.

Study point

Write a paragraph commenting on the importance of sex–role differentiation in the Functionalist account.

OTHER FUNCTIONALIST APPROACHES

Of course, not everyone in the Functionalist school agreed wholly with Parsons. Sociology has been characterised, throughout its history, by controversies and debates, and the sociology of families is no exception.

Murdock, for example, saw the family as performing four essential functions, namely sexual, economic, reproductive and educational (including socialisation of the young). He highlighted the sexual drive as a powerful impulse, and saw marriage as a means for satisfying and channelling it in a contained and controlled way. He also identified the economic co-operation between man and wife as important; the man's wage was a 'family wage' to be shared with other family members.

Goode preferred to talk about the *conjugal family*, based on marriage. He saw this as an 'ideal type' and recognised that real families cannot always be reduced to their nuclear core. He disagreed with Parsons that the nuclear family had evolved to 'fit' the needs of an industrialised economy. Instead, he took the view that a form of the family emphasising the husband–wife–child unit may well have been a *facilitating factor* for industrialisation, rather than the other way around, because it made social and geographical mobility easier and favoured 'achievement orientation'. Goode placed the family of modern Western industrialised nations into context and was aware of the complexities of social change.

Others in the Functionalist school have developed ideas based on more recent *empirical* studies of family life in Britain. Michael Young and Peter Wilmott began their comprehensive study of family life in the East End of London in the 1950s. They identified a number of ways in which family life was changing, and which challenged the traditional Functionalist model in some ways. Two main challenges to traditional Functionalist sociology emerged from their work. First, they documented instances where *extended* family structures persisted, providing material and emotional support in working–class communities, thereby questioning the emphasis previously placed on the isolated nuclear family form. They found numerous cases of inter–generational co–operation and support, largely facilitated through the activities of women as mothers and grandmothers, that challenged old ideas that the nuclear family was an isolated unit, largely free of kinship ties. Secondly, they found some evidence of the blurring of traditional roles divided along gender lines; for example, they found fathers participating in child care activities, thus challenging old ideas of a rigid, gender–based segregation of labour. They talked instead about the *symmetrical* family, in which there was an increasing tendency towards more sharing and a more equal relationship between the spouses.

Study point

Explain, in a few sentences, what Young and Wilmott meant by the symmetrical family.

Some sociologists presented a challenge to the mainstream functionalist view by pointing out that the State (education, health services, social services, therapeutic practice, etc.) is increasingly taking over many of the functions previously performed by families. But others disagreed. British sociologist, Ronald Fletcher, for example, argued that the functions of the family had increased in detail and importance. He took the view that educational and welfare provisions *enhanced* the functions of the family, rather than undermined them. For example, since the creation of the Welfare State after the Second World War, state services have made family members more aware of the importance of health and hygiene, and the responsibilities of child care, such that their role in relation to these issues has been heightened rather than reduced.

Like other Functionalists, however, Fletcher recognised some important changes as regards the economic function of the family. There is some agreement amongst sociologists that, in pre–industrial society, the family was an economic *unit of production*, in which all family members, including children, played a part. Families at that time were the main producers of both goods and services, and thus performed an important economic function in society. But, with the coming of industrialisation, the family was no longer the main economic unit in society; its function was replaced by waged labour, and families no longer produced, but received wages for work done outside the home.

Activity
Why have families become units of consumption? Work together with other students in your group to identify the main products that families consume.

Sociologists now argue that the primary economic function of the family is not production, but *consumption*; family groups now buy and consume the goods and services produced in the economy. The family remains an important economic unit, but in a different way; goods and services are now bought and consumed in the name of 'the family'; from ready–made meals, through washing machines and cars, to telecommunication services, the advertisers on our TV sets and in magazines clearly regard families as providing the main market for the goods and services they promote. Family income is expended largely on things for the family; to the traditional advertisements for family holidays and family cars we can now add 'it's good to talk' family communications. The media assist in the creation of family life–styles, from DIY kitchen cabinets to herbaceous borders. Families can now improve themselves by altering their homes and gardens.

Activity
Working in a group with other students, identify five TV advertisements that promote particular products for family consumption and discuss the images of the family that they portray.

CRITICS OF FUNCTIONALISM

Since the late 1960s, Functionalist views of the family have been intensely debated in sociology. Criticisms came from a range of quarters, as a result of which the Functionalist approach is no longer regarded as adequate to explain the complexities of contemporary family life. Criticisms of the Functionalist view began to emerge as other schools of thought in sociology, such as Marxism and Feminism, developed new theoretical frameworks for explaining family life.

	Table 3: *Key theorists, concepts and issues: Critical perspectives*	
KEY THEORISTS	KEY CONCEPTS	KEY ISSUES
F. Engels (Marxism)	Bourgeois family	What part does the family play in reproducing the capitalist system?
C. Delphy and D. Leonard (Marxism)	Capitalist mode of reproduction	Is the family oppressive to women?
	False consciousness	Is the nuclear family a product of industrialisation?
B. Friedan (Feminism)	Family as dysfunctional	Why are social problems commonly attributed to 'family breakdown'?
H. Gavron (Feminism)	Patriarchy Gender politics	
S. Firestone (Feminism)	Domestic labour	
A. Oakley (Feminism)	Social control	
C. Smart (Feminism)		
R.D. Laing (Anti–psychiatry)		
P. Laslett (History)		

The main influences behind the decline in popularity of Functionalist views of the family were:

- Marxism: This emphasised the part played by the family in reproducing and maintaining the capitalist system.
- Feminism: This approach challenged the Functionalist notion of the family as a 'haven' and instead identified it as a locus of oppression for women, and a site of violence and abuse.
- Anti–psychiatry: The Anti–psychiatry movement, in the 1960s and 70s, pointed to the demands and tensions of ordinary family life as instrumental in the production of mental illness.
- History: Some historians undermined the basic tenets of Functionalism by challenging the inevitability of the nuclear family and documenting instances of the continued existence of extended families in industrialised societies. They pointed to the importance of variation in family forms according to geographical location and social class (see chapter 4).

Together, these critical strands within sociology have seriously undermined the ideas of the Functionalist school.

MARXIST APPROACHES

Karl Marx himself paid little attention to the family; he was more concerned with analysing the relations between the economic base of society and its ideological superstructures. The contribution of Marxism to family sociology began, in 1884, with the work of Friedrich Engels, Marx's lifetime collaborator. Marxists emphasised the fundamental importance of the *mode of production* (in our society, this is the *capitalist* mode) for all social structures, institutions and relationships. They saw the *economic base* of society as fundamentally *determining*. Marxists analysed the family in terms of its relationship with the wider society, most particularly with its *economic base* and its *ideological superstructures*. Engels was also concerned to explain the *subjugation of women* under capitalist economies, and saw women's roles in the family as oppressive.

Engels focussed on what he called the *bourgeois family*. This term highlighted the way Marxists saw the family as a product of economic forces, that played an essential part in maintaining and reproducing social relations in capitalist society. For Marx, the capitalist mode of production was based on a fundamental antagonism between the class that owned and controlled the means of production (the *ruling–class*) and the class that worked for wages (the *proletariat*, or working–class), and which was exploited by the need to make profit. Engels' treatise on *The Origins of the Family, Private Property and the State*, linked the family firmly to the structures and mechanisms for maintaining the capitalist economy.

For Engels, a society's mode of production shaped what he called its *mode of reproduction*. The bourgeois family was what guaranteed the reproduction of capitalism. Engels documented the historical transitions in the mode of production from feudalism, through capitalism, to communism, and discussed the implications of these political and economic transitions for the changing forms and functions of the family, including their consequences for women. He argued that the *monogamous* nuclear family, male domination and the subjugation of women were linked to the emergence of capitalism, and more specifically to private property. For Engels, the bourgeois family was *patriarchal* in nature; it had arisen to guarantee male power, and was based on men's needs, in a system that valued private property, to be sure about questions of paternity for inheritance purposes. Hence, he argued, that the monogamous patriarchal nuclear family had developed as a system of reproduction suited to a particular mode of production.

Thus, the family was part of the superstructure of society that served the interests of the ruling–class. The contribution of Marxism to family sociology can be summarised in the following four main points:

- Through the socialisation of children, the family reproduces both labour power and the *false consciousness* (or ideology) which keeps the capitalist system going.
- Women perform unpaid labour in the home that would otherwise have to be paid for at a considerable cost to those who benefit from it. Women also constitute a reserve army of labour, available to be called upon when the economy requires it (such as in times of war).
- The family represents a 'haven' from the exploitation and alienation inherent in wage labour. But it is, itself, a source of exploitation and alienation for women.
- The family is a unit of consumption, that buys the goods and services produced by the capitalist economy.

Points of Evaluation
There have been a number of criticisms of the Marxist view:

1 Anthropologists and historians have pointed out that evidence from other societies and other historical periods does not support the assumptions Engels made about the origins of the family.
2 Others have pointed out that women's participation in employment in the late–modern world has hardly mitigated their substantial inequality, as Engels predicted, and that socialist and communist societies have not been free either of male domination or of nuclear families.
3 Nevertheless, the criticisms of Functionalism made by Marxist scholars have been instrumental in moving the debate forward, and in laying the groundwork for other critical approaches.

FEMINIST APPROACHES

The 1960s saw the emergence of what has been called the *second wave of feminism*, and many women sociologists increasingly brought feminist concerns and values to their academic work. Family sociology has been radically revived by the ideas of feminist sociologists. During the 1970s and 80s, feminist criticisms of more traditional approaches in family sociology burgeoned, challenging the basic tenets of Functionalism and highlighting the deficiencies of Marxism. Feminists identified the family as a site of contradictions, tensions and oppression. At this time, *domestic violence* and *child abuse* became more visible as social problems, previously hidden away in the private sphere of the family (see chapter 8). These issues highlighted the private isolated nuclear family, not as a functional unit, but as *dysfunctional*, particularly for women and children.

FEMINISTS IN SOCIOLOGY

Ann Oakley, in the 1970s, carried out a major empirical study of housework. She interviewed women about the work they did in the home, and documented the burdens that they carried and the contradictions they had to resolve between romanticised views of love and marriage and the hard physical labour involved in home–making and child care. Oakley's work was groundbreaking; prior to her study, sociology as a discipline had not concerned itself at all with such 'mundane' topics as what women did in the home. Rather, the things that women did were assumed to be so 'natural' as not to warrant sociological study. For a long time, feminist sociologists struggled to make women's real lives respectable objects for sociological study. In the 1980s, Oakley conducted a major research project on motherhood that succeeded in putting women's issues clearly on the map of family sociology.

LOVE AND MARRIAGE

Jessie Bernard argued that *gender* exerted a fundamental influence on how intimate relationships and marriage were experienced and perceived. She said that, within every marriage, there are two: his and hers. Women and men had different, and sometimes conflicting, needs and expectations in relation to marriage, and the consequences of marriage were different, according to gender. Men benefited more from marriage than women did. This is still reflected in health statistics; mortality and morbidity rates are lower for married men than for single men, whilst the reverse is true for women.

Carol Smart referred to marriage in terms of the 'ties that bind'. Her work highlighted the ways in which legal relationships and obligations are brought about by marriage, and that these are premised on a particular view of what women should 'naturally' do in the family. For her, marriage was less about love and romance, and more about duty and obligation.

Activity

What are the main arguments for and against the family being a 'haven in a heartless world'? Conduct a class debate on this issue.

DOMESTIC LABOUR

Feminists in the 1970s, particularly those of a Marxist persuasion, were instrumental in the recognition that women's unpaid work in the home has an economic value. *Christine Delphy* highlighted the part played by women's unwaged domestic labour in the maintenance of the capitalist economy. She argued that, not only were women a reserve army of labour, but also that their domestic work produced *surplus value*; as such, women were exploited economically by their traditional familial roles. *Eli Zaretsky* pointed out that capitalist ideology placed women outside the economy and relegated them instead to the private sphere of the family where their work and their contribution to the capitalist economy was rendered invisible. She argued that the ideological separation of 'the public' and 'the private', of the political from the personal, obscured the fact that the family was an important material base for the production of the kinds of citizens needed by a capitalist democracy. For her, the family was important because of the links between our inner selves, our emotional needs, and broader economic and political structures.

More recently, *Delphy and Leonard,* also working in the Marxist tradition, characterised the family itself as an economic system. For them, domestic groups are not just collections of individuals bound together by affection or kinship, but are part of a whole system of hierarchically organised labour relations – a kind of microcosm of the capitalist social system. They argued that oppressions occur within families because subordinates are dependants who do not own their own labour power in the same way that male heads of households own theirs.

The issue of domestic labour can also be usefully examined in the context of the interrelations among family, social class and ethnicity. Sociological work has demonstrated the ways in which the careers of middle–class people have been facilitated by the domestic labour of other women; women from other social groups who cook, clean and provide childcare services, enabling wealthier women and men to pursue paid work outside the home.

Activity
List at least four sources of criticism for the Functionalist position. Decide which offers the most powerful criticism, and give reasons for your choice.

Points of Evaluation

- One of the strongest criticisms of the Functionalist school to have emerged from within feminism is the idea that the family is instrumental in the system of social control in our society.
- *Barrett and MacIntosh* saw Functionalism as contributing to an ideology of the family, whose role it was to maintain the *status quo*, including the oppression of women. They advocated *deconstructing* the family, to expose its internal tensions and contradictions, and to expose the role played by the family in the processes of social regulation of citizens.
- The ideology of the nuclear family assists in social control by positioning, as deviant or undesirable, non–nuclear forms, such as lone–parents and gay couples; difference and diversity is denied validity.

- The language of 'roles' in the Functionalist account participates in social control by creating an ideology in which roles appear to be natural and inevitable, and thus the possibility of change is minimised.
- The feminist approaches perhaps have made their greatest contribution to family sociology in drawing attention to the importance of the family in relation to the social relations of the broader sex/gender system in society.
- Until recently, much work in family sociology tended to refer to *the* family, but it is now commonplace to refer, instead, to *families*. In this way, it becomes possible to acknowledge diversity and to move beyond the biological notions inherent in the idea of a predominant and natural family form.
- The primacy of the stereotypical nuclear family can be understood as an ideology, that links families to social regulatory mechanisms.
- Our institutions, laws and welfare policies are based around a stereotypical nuclear family; this is not because it *is* the norm, but in order that it *shall* be the norm.
- This approach is particularly characteristic of *New Right* thinking. Here, a pessimistic view of contemporary families is maintained.
- A variety of social problems such as youth crime, teenage pregnancy and educational failure are attributed to the 'breakdown' of families and the demise of family values.
- It is not uncommon to find this kind of thinking underlying the speeches of politicians, and to find such marginal groups as single parents being 'blamed' for a range of social ills. Underlying these sentiments is an idealisation of the 'traditional' family and a desire to return to 'the good old days'. What we can see here are ideologies at work, where ideas about families are being mobilised to address broader social problems.

SUMMARY

The Functionalist approach identified the family as an integral part of the social system and as the cornerstone of society. Functionalists argued that the family performed functions that were essential for the smooth running of society. These included the socialisation of children and the stabilisation of adult personalities. It saw the *isolated nuclear* family as having a *functional fit* with the needs of the industrialised economy. The Functionalist approach assumed a division of labour, both in the home (the *private* sphere) and outside of it (the *public* sphere), along gender lines.

Functionalist sociology of the family was subjected to criticism from the late 1960s onwards. The main criticisms came from Marxism, feminism and anti-psychiatry. Marxist critics emphasised the role played by the family in maintaining the capitalist system. Feminist critics focussed mainly on gender issues, and argued that families could be oppressive to women, and were often the locus of violence and abuse. These were seen as expressions of *patriarchal power*, in which society condoned men's domination of women and children. Anti-psychiatry was popular in the 1970s. The anti–psychiatrists argued that mental illness was socially produced, and they identified dysfunctional family relationships and patterns of communication in the genesis of mental illness.

The popularity of Functionalism has declined considerably under the weight of these criticisms. Feminist approaches to the sociology of the family have now become mainstream, and the issue of gender is now recognised by all sociologists as central to the understanding of families.

STUDY GUIDES

Group activities

1 In your group, construct ten questions to enable you to identify what domestic tasks are done by women and men. Use your questionnaire to conduct some research. What do you conclude about the ways in which domestic labour is currently organised?
2 Identify the arguments for and against the idea that stable families are necessary for the smooth running of society. Conduct a class debate on the issue.
3 In your group, consider what kinds of evidence might be produced to support the argument that families can be dangerous places.

Practice questions

Item A

The most important implication of this view is that the functions of the family in a highly differentiated society are not to be interpreted as functions directly on behalf of the society, but on behalf of personality. If, as some psychologists seem to assume, the essentials of human personality were determined biologically, independently of involvement in social systems, there would be no need for families, since reproduction as such does not require family organisation. It is because the human personality is not 'born' but must be 'made' through the socialisation process that in the first instance families are necessary. They are 'factories' which produce human personalities. But at the same time, even once produced, it cannot be assumed that the human personality would remain stable in the respects which are vital to social functioning, if there were not mechanisms of stabilisation which were organically integrated with the socialisation process. We therefore suggest that the basic and irreducible functions of the family are two: first, the primary socialisation of children so that they can truly become members of the society into which they have been born; second, the stabilisation of the adult personalities of the population of the society.

Talcott Parsons, (1980) 'The American family: its relations to personality and social structure', in T. Parsons and R.F. Bales, *Family, Socialisation and Interaction Process*, Free Press, 1955, reprinted in M. Anderson (ed.) *Sociology of the Family*, Penguin, pp192–193.

Item B

What a feminist social scientist saw when she looked at the family in the early 1970s, therefore, was a very radical questioning of a woman's place within it. Further disclosure of men's domestic violence against women, of their sexual coercion and abuse of children in the home, and a general control over resources and decision–making, all contributed both to feed feminist calls for a woman–centred orientation in the social sciences and to fan feminist fears of the potential dangers of family life for women (and children) throughout the 1970s, so firmly hidden in the all pervasive familial ideology of the satisfactions of hearth and home. What this meant within feminist theory was that the family could no longer be analysed as a homogeneous unit. Its internal structures and functions, and its wider economic, political and ideological significance, all needed to be untangled to reveal the power relations of men over women, and the patterns of individual costs or benefits operating along gender and generational lines.

Lynne Segal, (1994) 'A feminist looks at the family', in J. Muncie et al (eds.) *Understanding the Family*, Sage, p301.

1 With reference to Item A, explain why the Functionalists saw the family as essential for social stability.
2 With reference to Item A and elsewhere, explain the Functionalist idea that the nuclear family 'fit' the needs of an industrialised economy.
3 With reference to Item B and elsewhere, describe the contribution made by feminist scholars to family sociology and evaluate its significance.
4 With reference to elsewhere, list FIVE sources of criticism of the Functionalist approach.
5 With reference to elsewhere, what kinds of evidence could be used to show that families are units of consumption?

Coursework suggestions

1 Critically evaluate the contribution of the Functionalist school to family sociology.

2 Explain and evaluate the contribution that feminist scholars have made to family sociology.

3 Describe Engels' theory on the *Origin of the Family, Private Property and the State* and critically evaluate his contribution to family sociology.

4

HISTORICAL PERSPECTIVES ON HOUSEHOLDS AND FAMILIES

Introduction

HISTORICAL PERSPECTIVES IN family sociology are important for several reasons. First, a historical approach helps us to contextualise contemporary social phenomena and puts our current concerns into a broader framework of understanding. Secondly, it enables us to investigate the debates around the question of the relationship between family and social structures and social change. Thirdly, it permits us to examine arguments about the functions of families and how these might have altered over time. Finally, it is possible to challenge a number of *myths* about the family with reference to historical work.

Table 4: *Key theorists, concepts and issues: Functionalism*		
KEY THEORISTS & THEORIES	KEY CONCEPTS	KEY ISSUES
P. Laslett Demographic approach L. Stone Sentiments approach M. Anderson Household Economics approach W. Seccombe	Industrialisation Open lineage family Restricted patriarchal nuclear family Closed domesticated nuclear family Symmetrical family	What can history tell us about families? Do particular family forms correspond with particular historical periods? Did industrialisation bring the nuclear family into being?

	Companionate marriage	Is the nuclear family peculiar to industrialised societies?
		How did the modern family come to be?
		What are the characteristics of the modern family?

As we have seen, the Functionalist school took the view that the nuclear family was peculiar to industrialised society, and that there was a functional and structural 'fit' between this particular family form and the industrial capitalist economy. In other words, industrialisation was seen as *causing* fundamental changes in the structure and functions of families. These assumptions have been challenged by historical work. In this chapter, we examine what prominent historians have had to say about the family in previous epochs.

There are two main elements to traditional 'myths' about the family in history that may be challenged with reference to historical evidence:

- The pre–industrial family was large and extended but, with industrialisation, it became smaller and more isolated.
- The pre–industrial family was primarily an economic unit, engaged in subsistence production, but the modern family has lost its economic functions and instead is primarily a relational unit concerned with support, care and personal fulfilment.

Three main approaches to family history will be discussed:

1 The demographic approach, associated with the work of Peter Laslett
2 The sentiments approach, associated with the work of Lawrence Stone
3 The household economics approach, associated with the work of Michael Anderson

| *Study points* |

Give three reasons why studying families from an historical perspective is important. What are the myths about the family that history helps us to challenge?

THE DEMOGRAPHIC APPROACH TO FAMILY HISTORY

The work of *Peter Laslett* and his fellow demographic historians at Cambridge has been extremely important in questioning the Functionalist notion that the process of industrialisation in Britain brought about a fundamental change in family structure, from extended to nuclear. Laslett questioned the existence of a typical extended family in the pre–industrial period and argued, instead, that the mean household size remained more or less constant at an average of 4.75 people from the 16th century, through industrialisation, until the end of the 19th century, when a steady decline set in to a figure of about 3 per household in contemporary censuses. Thus Laslett's work denies the Functionalist view that the nuclear family came into being after the industrial revolution. He found that the pre–industrial household was no more likely to include two or more generations than is the present day household. On this basis, it has been said that the 'extended' family of 'the good old days' is probably little more than a myth and is not supported by historical evidence. A further conclusion that may be drawn from Laslett's work is that the nuclear family seems to have a longer history than has previously been supposed.

Study point
What is the significance of Laslett's finding that families in past times were smaller than had previously been thought?

Laslett's work also points to the importance of 'continuities' in history, as opposed to an emphasis on change. *Wally Seccombe*, however, has argued convincingly against the 'continuity' thesis and finds that families changed in far-reaching ways in the transition from feudalism to capitalism. The main changes, according to Seccombe, may be summarised as follows:

- As families became increasingly separated from the means of production, they lost the capacity to transmit productive property, and the means for subsistence, to the next generation. Instead, livelihoods were secured in the labour market rather than in the productive family unit.
- With the separation of labourers from the means of production, their households ceased to be centres of commodity production. The only thing families had for sale was their members' labour power.
- As households ceased to make any goods to consume, neighbourly exchange declined and the domestic division of labour along gender lines was intensified.

- As households and workplaces became increasingly separate, the residential, private sphere became a relatively autonomous domain, divorced in important ways from the public world, although constrained by the broader patterns of work and leisure of the capitalist economic system.
- Domestic service and formal apprenticeship, as stepping–stones to adulthood, assisted by families, were replaced by compulsory education provided by the State.
- Marriage lost its character as a property transaction and a social relationship between two families, and a new ideology of marriage based on love emerged.

Seccombe also challenges the Functionalist view that the industrial revolution was instrumental in bringing nuclear families into being. He argues that, instead, the dominant form of the family in Western Europe itself provided an impetus to the breakthrough of industrial capitalism. Seccombe's work has been widely regarded as offering a sustained challenge to Laslett's thesis.

Laslett's work has made such an impact in family sociology that it is important to evaluate it carefully:

- What kind of data is Laslett's analysis based on?
- Does Laslett's account tell us the whole story?

Laslett's work was based mainly on data from such sources as census returns and parish records, and was concerned with demographic changes such as birth and death rates, and household size and composition. The data were subjected to sophisticated computer analysis. These data have several limitations, as Michael Anderson, another historian, points out. The limitations may be summarised as follows:

- The listings in census returns and parish registers used by Laslett were prepared for administrative purposes, so it is not known whether such listings were full and comprehensive or the extent to which they were incomplete.
- Community–level statistics give only a 'snap–shot' of family life that cannot capture either cyclical changes in individual families, or variability related to, for example, social class or geographical location.
- The issue of the relationship between 'household' and 'family' cannot be addressed with reference to the kind of analysis Laslett used.
- Statistics tell us nothing about people's lives and experiences, and the meanings of family life for them.

THE 'SENTIMENTS' APPROACH TO FAMILY HISTORY

What Anderson refers to as the 'sentiments' school poses questions, not about household size and composition, but about the meaning and significance of familial relationships in times past. It moves away from the premises of Functionalism because its focus is on neither structure nor function, but on the processes of social change that have led to the present day. This approach is exemplified in the work of *Lawrence Stone*. His work goes beyond the debate about the assumed transition from extended to nuclear families, and the significance of the industrial revolution, and looks instead at broader shifts and patterns, at relations within families, and at relations between the family and the State. The sources for such historical work include such things as diaries, contemporary accounts, religious and imaginative literature, and artefacts such as domestic architecture, toys and paintings.

Stone traces the historical evolution of the family between 1500 and 1800 and sees it as comprised in three main stages:

THE OPEN LINEAGE FAMILY, 1450–1630

The first stage of the family's evolution, he says, was characterised by extensive kinship and community ties and a relative lack of close relationships within families. Marriages, at least in the higher echelons of society, were primarily social and economic contracts, and family groupings were held together by shared economic interests rather than emotional bonds. Families were hierarchically organised, with the father (or *paterfamilias*) at the top and women and children subject to his authority. Stone argues that, by today's standards, the open lineage family was bleak and impersonal.

THE RESTRICTED PATRIARCHAL NUCLEAR FAMILY, 1550–1700

By the middle of the 16th century, there were changes afoot. Stone argues that a declining significance of lineage, kin and community was replaced by an increasing loyalty to State and church. The father, however, remained the undisputed 'head' of the family. Stone sees, in this period, the boundaries of family becoming more clearly defined, as the importance of affectional ties begins to increase. He links these developments to wider social changes, including Protestant reform in the church. Poorer people came under increasing pressure to formalise their unions by marriage as part of a wider attempt morally to educate the poor.

CLOSED DOMESTICATED NUCLEAR FAMILY, 1640–1800

The third stage of the evolution of the nuclear family is linked, in Stone's view, with the rise of the philosophy of *affective individualism* that accompanied industrialisation and the consolidation of the capitalist economy. Thus he identified a tendency towards an interest in 'the individual', and demands for personal autonomy, individual achievement and a right to privacy; these were the cultural values associated with the advent of the capitalist economic system. They resulted in smaller, nuclear families, relatively isolated from kin and community, and characterised by strong emotional bonds (including love and romance as a basis for marriage) within the nuclear unit. Interestingly, Stone also argues that it was during this period that children were first identified as a special status group, distinct from adults. This is supported by work on the history of childhood.

Thus, Stone characterises three main family types which he associates with the particular material and cultural circumstances of different historical periods. Not all historians, however, would agree that it is possible to straightforwardly link particular family forms with particular historical periods. For example, Anderson in Britain and Flandrin in France both emphasise the importance of geographical variations in family patterns and household composition.

THE MAIN POINTS OF THE 'SENTIMENTS' APPROACH TO FAMILY HISTORY

Anderson identifies five essential points of the 'sentiments' approach, which can be summarised as follows:

- The segregation of the conjugal unit, with an emphasis on isolation, privacy and domesticity. That is, over the four centuries covered by Stone's work, the family increasingly becomes an isolated, private unit based around marriage. The change began, first, among the upper classes, but by the 19th century, an emerging ideology of 'home sweet home' was present in working–class families too.
- Changing attitudes to interpersonal relationships: families lose their economic and contractual focus and become, instead, the locus for close, emotional relationships, and the pursuit of individual fulfilment and happiness.
- Spouse selection: expressive considerations gradually replace instrumental criteria as the basis for mate selection. Romantic and sexual love, previously separated from marriage, becomes more closely linked with it.

- Parenthood and childhood: new constructions of parenthood and childhood have emerged at different stages in the evolution of the family.
- The motor for social change: the sentiments school stresses the primary significance of meanings and attitudes, in stark contrast to the Functionalist emphasis on social structures and the Marxist emphasis on the mode of production.

Activity
Explain, in your own words, the significance of a 'sentiments' approach to family history.

Points of Evaluation

Anderson is critical of the 'sentiments' school, and regards the evidential problems it raises as almost insuperable.

- History is, of course, always an interpretive activity, and complete objectivity is always difficult to achieve.
- The quest for historical truth is rendered the more difficult when using such sources as diaries and other personal documents as tend to be relied on by scholars in the sentiments school.
- Interpretation of these kinds of data necessarily involve speculation and imagination, which some scholars find unacceptable.

Anderson's own preferred approach is one based on household economics.

Study point
What does Anderson mean when he says that there are difficult evidential problems associated with the work of the 'sentiments' approach to family history?

THE HOUSEHOLD ECONOMICS APPROACH

The primary concern of this approach is with the social processes that underlie family structures and familial attitudes in the past. Anderson's sources include documents describing property holdings, property utilisation and transmission, employment records, family budgets, and contemporary descriptions of working practices. Drawing on these data, he attempts to understand family life, identifying the structural influences on family behaviours that arise in the wider society and in the economy.

Anderson's early work was on the Lancashire textile industry. He uncovers complex relationships between industrialisation and changing family forms that challenge the equation of the industrial revolution and the emergence of the nuclear family. He argues that, in Lancashire, the extended family actually became *more common* in the early days of industrialisation. This may have been so because it was the arrangement that made most financial sense in uncertain conditions, rather than because it was a preferred way of life.

In addition, Anderson argues that the process of industrialisation was not nearly so disruptive of existing family patterns and value systems as has often been supposed. On the contrary, Anderson's work shows the extent to which traditional attitudes persisted and influenced the strategies adopted by families whose members became involved in factory work. Employers, too, adopted strategies for labour recruitment that, to some extent, respected traditional value systems and took account of local conditions.

Points of Evaluation

Anderson's work thus stresses the ways in which historical evolution is made up of both *change* and *continuity*; it demonstrates the multi-dimensional nature of the social world, of which the family is but one part.

- It illustrates how changes in one dimension are not necessarily accompanied by parallel changes in another, and how, at times, conflicts emerge, for example between material conditions and dominant social values.
- Anderson's work also reminds us of the importance of geographical location and local context; it is not possible to assume that, throughout the whole of Britain, the same factors that Anderson identified in Lancashire were operating to shape family life.
- The household economics approach demonstrates how the various strategies used by families are understandable in the context of the world in which they lived and how, in turn, local conditions responded to the needs and skills of local families.

Activity

Briefly describe and then evaluate the 'household economics' approach to family history. Identify its merits and its limitations.

The three perspectives on family history that we have reviewed in this chapter each present a different picture of families in times past. Each constitutes a different focus, and each contributes new knowledge and ideas to the debate. It is clear that the issue of family size and household composition is a more complex one than the Functionalists envisaged in the earlier days of family sociology, but it is also important to recognise the significant contribution made by Functionalism. If history is an interpretive discipline, then it necessarily generates disagreements, and is likely to thrive on debate.

THE RISE OF THE MODERN FAMILY

Sociologists characterise the modern family as egalitarian, symmetrical, and based on a 'companionate' marriage. As we have seen, historically, three broad features of this family have emerged that distinguish it from earlier family forms:

- Intensified affective emotional bonding between members of the nuclear core to the exclusion of neighbours, kin and community
- A strong sense of individual autonomy and of the right to freedom, choice and the pursuit of happiness
- A weakening of the association of sexual pleasure with sin and guilt, and an open acknowledgement of the desire for physical intimacy.

Activity

Identify three main features that characterise the modern family and which distinguish it from earlier family forms.

THE SYMMETRICAL FAMILY

When contemporary sociologists talk about the 'symmetrical' family or the 'companionate' marriage, they are referring, primarily, to the issue of relationships within families. As we have seen, those in the 'sentiments' school placed great emphasis on this topic. In this section, we shall be exploring a paradox: how is it that our high divorce rate is accompanied by a continuing faith in marriage? Recent social attitudes surveys in Britain indicate that marriage remains valued and that the ideal of monogamy is as prominent as it has ever been. Yet, the statistical evidence tells us that few marriages are likely to last. How should we explain this paradox? To begin to answer this question requires that we consider the rise of the modern family from an historical perspective.

HISTORICAL PERSPECTIVE

The novelist and social commentator, Daniel Defoe, writing in 1727, pointed out that any transition to love, as a basis for marriage, would have to be accompanied by a change in power relations between men and women. The love of a wife, and her subjection within the home, he saw as basically incompatible. By 1740, the popular literature of the time had begun to portray marriage as a state of domestic bliss, and the wife as the 'bosom friend' of her husband. Current familial ideologies emphasise similar things, and they are therefore familiar to us (even as we recognise that realities are sometimes very different); it is therefore important to appreciate the relative historical recency of these ideas. The civil wars of the mid 17th century had stimulated many women into political activity, and some of the early feminists at this time demanded equality with men. Herein lie the historical roots of contemporary ideals of the companionate marriage and symmetrical families.

These ideals portray marriage as, primarily, a site for emotional closeness, physical intimacy, sexual satisfaction, companionship, equal partnership between spouses and, importantly, for individual self–actualisation. Marriage came to be seen as a relationship offering not just love, affection and a sexual relationship, but also a shared private world in which spouses share tasks, spend much of their leisure time together and pursue goals of self–fulfilment. This is the pattern of domestic life that continues to dominate in the industrialised world, although there are some signs of change that we will discuss in more detail in chapter 6.

Activity
List the features that characterise the 'companionate' marriage.

COMPANIONATE MARRIAGE

After the Second World War, the companionate marriage received a new impetus. The War created a climate of fear and uncertainty and, in its aftermath, rapid social change and a widespread concern to restore stability and prosperity. Central to the post–war efforts to reconstruct society was a desire to consolidate family life; there had been a worrying peak in divorce rates as the war ended. Efforts were directed towards environmental, economic and social reconstruction, aimed at providing a society more conducive to stable family life. This emphasis on the family can be understood against the backdrop of a concern with the low birth rate in the 1940s, leading to pronatalist policies which encouraged women to have children and to rear them according to the latest psychological principles. These policies, accompanied as they were by powerful ideologies about the vulnerability of children and their need for a physically and psychologically available mother, also served the purpose of bringing women out of the munitions factories and off the land, where they had worked through the war years, back into the home where their husbands and children needed them. Thus we see, at this time, a proliferation of psychological theories that stress the crucial importance of mothers for normal child development, and of stable families for society as a whole.

Study point
What is meant by 'pronatalism'?

A Royal Commission on Population reported in 1949. It recommended that there be larger family allowances (now called Child Benefit), family services (for example, home helps), NHS advice and assistance with reproductive issues, and measures to tackle housing shortages. All of these provisions were designed to promote family life in material and ideological ways. The fostering of close emotional bonds within the family was a central feature of post–war reconstruction.

However, throughout this period, there remained an ambivalence about gender equality. As Finch and Summerfield argue, however, the ideal of the companionate marriage produced contradictory pressures; men and women were seen as equal partners, but there was concern lest too much emphasis on equality should undermine other features of family life seen as essential for stability. For example, tensions around the sexual division of domestic labour were resolved by an ideology that saw men's and women's contribution to the family as different but equal. But, as feminists were later to observe, the resolution of these tensions placed particular strains on women in the family. The Royal Commission on Divorce, in 1955, expressed concern about the rising divorce rate and recognised that marriage itself was being exposed to new strains. Its recommendations for better education, marriage guidance and sanctions to encourage better responsibility for children have echoes in today's debates; as today, they failed to address the central tensions within the companionate ideal itself.

Study point
Why did the 'companionate' marriage receive new impetus after the Second World War?

Points of Evaluation

Sociologists have argued that, perhaps, the companionate ideal contains within it, the seeds of its own destruction.

- The most important tensions are those around gender equality in the family. As feminist sociologists have repeatedly shown, for many women, the experience of family life can be isolating, depressing, unfulfilling and unrewarding. Men, as husbands and as fathers, may help in the home but, except in a small minority of families, they do not take responsibility for housework or child care, which is left to women.

- The advent of household technologies, such as washing machines and fridges, rather than having alleviated the burden on women, has had the effect of altering expectations and raising standards, such that women spend as much, if not more, time on household tasks as they did before. This is so, even in dual earner families; Hochschild talks about 'the double shift' that women in such families perform.

- There are further tensions within the companionate marriage around the ideals of sharing and individual autonomy. People get married expecting to find self–fulfilment in their chosen relationship but, as Bernard has argued, this is especially difficult for women.

- The isolation and privacy of the nuclear family has been identified by feminist sociologists as little more than a licence for men to dominate, or even abuse, women and children (see chapter 9).

- Autonomy and self–fulfilment are ideals upon which great premium is placed in the late modern world, but these ideals are likely to clash, not only with the realities of family life (for example, the need to 'put children first') but also with the material constraints on housing, child care, secure job opportunities, and so on.

- Ideals of self–fulfilment also clash with ideals of sharing. True sharing is difficult unless the two partners are equal and sociologists have pointed out that, despite women's formal legal equality with men, they still suffer from a range of substantial inequalities, many of which are centred upon their positions as wives and mothers in families.

These kinds of arguments form the basis for sociologists' views that the companionate marriage contains internal contradictions; the seeds of its own destruction. Yet there can be no doubt that the companionate ideal, as an ideal, lives on. This is clearly documented by sociological work on marriage and also appears in surveys of social attitudes. At the same time, Britain experiences one of the highest divorce rates in the industrialised world, testimony to the fact that the companionate ideal is difficult to realise in practice. To return to our paradox: how is it that so many people seem to retain a faith in marriage and at the same time we see evidence of the likelihood of marriage breakdown? Sociologists would say the answer lies in the unrealistic expectations that attend the companionate ideal, that there are fundamental tensions between ideals and realities of gender equality, and between the desires and the realities of family life, and between the pursuit of self–fulfilment as an individual goal and the material and relational demands that families make upon us.

SUMMARY

Historical perspectives on families help us to contextualise contemporary social phenomena and to put current concerns into a broader framework. Historical evidence also helps us to challenge some of the myths about families in past times. The Functionalists saw the process of industrialisation as causing changes in family structure and function, and believed that industrialisation was responsible for a transition from large extended families to smaller, more isolated, nuclear ones. The Functionalist account has been challenged by historical work.

Historian Michael Anderson identifies three main approaches to family history: the demographic approach, the sentiments approach and the household economics approach. The demographic approach is mainly associated with the work of Peter Laslett and his colleagues. Using such sources as census data and parish records, Laslett found that household sizes in pre–industrial times were generally smaller than had previously been supposed, thus challenging the idea that families changed from being 'extended' to 'nuclear' in any straightforward way.

The sentiments approach is associated with the work of Lawrence Stone. He was interested, not just in structural changes, but also in the significance of relationships in past times. His sources included diaries, literature and domestic artefacts. Stone saw the evolution of the family between 1500 and 1800 as comprised in three main stages, with overlap between them. He characterised three main family types that were associated with the material and cultural circumstances of each historical period. His work offers an explanation of how the modern, isolated, nuclear family came into being over at least four centuries, in the context of changing social and political circumstances, and changing ideologies.

The household economics approach is associated with the work of Michael Anderson. He was interested in the social processes that underlie family structures and attitudes. His sources included documents related to property, employment practices and family budgets. His work shows that geographical location is important; family patterns in Lancashire were linked to particular local conditions of the textile industries, and represented arrangements that made financial sense to both employers and employees in that particular community.

Sociologists have debated whether the history of the family is best characterised in terms of change or in terms of continuities. The work generated by the three main approaches to family history does not enable us to draw this debate to a definitive conclusion. Instead, it reminds us of the complexity and the multi–dimensional nature of historical processes. Change in one dimension of social life is not always accompanied by parallel changes in others, and there can be tensions and contradictions, as some aspects of life change more quickly than others, and as some traditional arrangements show more resistance than others to fundamental change.

A historical approach can reveal to us the social and economic roots of contemporary family patterns. Modern families are said to be more symmetrical and egalitarian than in times past, and to be characterised by more intensive affective bonding to the exclusion of wider kin and community. In addition, individuals today have a stronger sense of their own autonomy and personal freedom than did our ancestors. The modern family is said to be based around the companionate marriage, where marriage offers love, security, sexual satisfaction and companionship. Historical work shows the roots of this in the philosophy of affective individualism in the 18th century. But it received new impetus in Britain after the Second World War, as government policies were designed to reconstruct families and society after the disruptions of the War.

Many commentators have suggested that the companionate marriage is an unstable ideal. This is because it is based on notions of egalitarianism and sharing that are undermined by continuing gender inequalities. They also identify a fundamental tension between commitment to the family group as a whole, and the emphasis on marriage as the locus for individual self–actualisation. Nevertheless, it is true to say that as ideals, the symmetrical family and the companionate marriage remain strong influences on the expectations people have in family life.

Group activities

1 In your group, devise a questionnaire of ten items to ascertain the values that people attach to marriage. Use your questionnaire to conduct some research. Do your findings support the idea that modern marriage is 'companionate'?
2 Conduct a class debate: This house believes that the pre–industrial family was large and extended but, with industrialisation, it became smaller and more isolated.

Practice questions

Item A

Mr and Mrs Trickett, who were married in 1955, had total role segregation. He went out to work and she stayed at home; Mr Trickett believing that a woman's place was in the home. He did not help with the housework and in this area there was clearly no sharing. Their degree of role separation could…have been related to a closely knit network of social relationships, but this was not the case. The couple were resolute in their determination to keep themselves to themselves, and had few contacts with relations or neighbours. However, they spent all their leisure time together, sometimes touring the countryside on their motorbike. They could clearly be described as having shared leisure and they were good companions. Mrs Trickett was, nevertheless, extremely isolated, lacking during the day the companionship of other women, whether in the street or in her home. Some marriages were never companionate. Others started thus, with a professed belief in sharing and team–work, but changed, usually with the arrival of children, which affected patterns both of work and leisure. Earlier companionship was too often destroyed, as was the woman's chance of equality with her husband in the labour market. Finch and Summerfield concluded that, in the 1940s and 1950s, the ideal of companionate marriage had many benefits for the husband but did not work to the advantage of the wife, and that indeed the ideal placed many pressures upon her.

Elizabeth Roberts, 1995, *Women and Families: An Oral History, 1940–1970*, Blackwell, p105.

Item B

Did patriarchy wither away in the transition to capitalism, to be replaced by companionate unions, with egalitarian relations between spouses and permissive child–rearing practices? Many scholars have written as if this were the case … Lawrence Stone, in *The Family, Sex and Marriage in England, 1500–1800*, traces the decline of the patriarchal family and the rise of affective individualism among the aristocracy in the late seventeenth and eighteenth centuries. Peter Laslett, in *The World We have Lost*, covering the same period for the popular classes in England, describes a similar evolution … Edward Shorter, in *The Making of the Modern Family*, perceives a veritable sexual revolution at the end of the eighteenth century, led by young proletarian women, with the eclipse of the patriarchal control of courtship and mate selection…Finally, sociologists Michael Young and Peter Wilmott, in *The Symmetrical Family*, concur with the historians' consensus portraying the demise of patriarchy, although they see the decisive shift to companionate marriage occurring much later, in the current century. Feminists have taken strong exception to this benign and complacent view of more or less continuous progress from 'the Bad Old Days' … towards equality in modern families. Undoubtedly there have been major changes in the scope and form of patriarchal authority in the passage from inheritance–based peasant families to the modern nuclear families of urban wage-earners….But these alternations have not entailed the terminal demise of patriarchal authority so much as its intergenerational truncation and the reconstruction of spousal hierarchy on new material foundations.

Wally Seccombe, 1992, *A Millennium of Family Change*, Verso, pp242–243.

Item C

Before systematic historical study of the family began, various social science disciplines had generated their own myths and grand theories about continuities and changes in family behaviour in the past. Sociologists in particular argued that, in pre–industrial societies, the dominant household form had contained an extended family, often involving three co–resident generations, and that the 'modern' family, characterised by a nuclear household structure, family limitations, the spacing of children, and population mobility, was the product of industrialisation. Associated with these generalisations was also the popular myth that industrialisation destroyed family harmony and community life. But historical research on the family has provided a perspective on change over time as well as on family behaviour within specific social and cultural contexts in discrete time periods. It has led to the rejection of these assumptions and to the resulting questioning of the role of industrialisation as a major watershed for American and European history.

Tamara Hareven, 1994, 'Recent research on the history of the family', in Michael Drake (ed.) *Time, Family and Community*, Blackwell, p14.

1 Referring to Item A and elsewhere, what were the defining features of 'companionate' marriage?

2 Referring to Item B and elsewhere, describe the main changes that historians have identified as significant in the development of companionate marriage up to the Second World War.

3 Referring to Item A and elsewhere, describe the social conditions after the Second World War that underpinned the consolidation of the companionate ideal.

4 Referring to Items A and B and elsewhere, list the main reasons that sociologists have suggested for the inherent instability of companionate marriage.

5 Referring to Item C and elsewhere, evaluate the claim that the emergence of industrial capitalism was instrumental in the development of the nuclear family.

Coursework suggestions

1 Write an essay entitled: 'What is most important in the history of the family, change or continuity?'

2 'The companionate marriage contains within it the seeds of its own destruction'. Discuss.

5

DIFFERENCE AND DIVERSITY

Introduction

FAMILIES IN CONTEMPORARY Britain exhibit a bewildering diversity of forms and patterns. The dominant ideal of the nuclear family is challenged by the existence of a variety of domestic arrangements, including gay and lesbian families, lone–mothers and lone–fathers, foster families, traveller families, cohabiting couples, step families, families with children born of assisted reproductive technologies, surrogacy arrangements and children in care. These families clearly depart from the stereotype of two married parents with their genetically related dependent children, but they are nevertheless families for all that. These families raise the spectre of difference and remind us that a unitary concept of family is inadequate to capture diverse realities. Either by choice, or otherwise, people do not always find themselves in families that correspond to the white, heterosexual, nuclear, middle–class norm.

Increasingly, sociologists recognise that families can be the *families we choose*; families without a partner of the opposite sex, or with children who may not be biologically related, are increasingly common, and remind us of the extent to which lived realities of family life depart from the norms that society prescribes for us. In this chapter we examine the issues of difference and diversity as they relate to family life. We focus on two main issues: homosexual families and families in minority ethnic groups.

Table 5: *Key concepts and issues*	
KEY CONCEPTS	KEY ISSUES
Diversity Gay and lesbian families Lone–parent families Foster families Step families Cohabiting couples Families we choose Families in minority ethnic groups	What are the defining features of the dominant 'norm' of family life? How are families that depart from the 'norm' portrayed? Why has it been difficult for sociologists to focus on diversity in their study of families? Does the sexual orientation of one's parents make a difference to the ways in which children develop? Is it possible to characterise families in minority ethnic communities as being of particular types?

REPRESENTATIONS OF FAMILY

Families that depart from the nuclear norm are often portrayed as deviant or undesirable in some way. For example, children of divorced parents (of 'broken homes') are seen as susceptible to particular kinds of 'damage' that can result in a propensity for crime and delinquency. There are no research studies that support this, but it is a powerful ideology, apt to be invoked from time to time. Yet statistics show that, at any given time, the number of families who conform to the nuclear stereotype of married parents and their biological children are on the decrease, whilst children born to lone–mothers and to cohabiting couples are on the increase. The married couple with their children is a relatively rare form of household, constituting less than a quarter of all households.

Departures from the nuclear ideal are common, yet they remain subject to stigma and denigration, and are often blamed for a range of social problems. A few years ago, for example, the death of two year old Jamie Bulger provided an opportunity for wide sections of the press to inject new life into ideas about the horrors of broken families, lone parenthood and fatherless families. The two boys convicted of the murder were alternately portrayed as either evil demons or the unfortunate victims of parental selfishness and irresponsibility. Society's collective wrath and horror was directed towards these boys' already suffering families, as though they were somehow to blame for what happened. The families were seen as having failed in their primary duty to produce decent citizens of their children; they were seen as deviant and 'un–whole–some', the sort of families that threaten social stability and cohesion through their departures from the nuclear norm.

JAMIE BULGER'S FUNERAL

Activity

Non–traditional families tend to be blamed for a range of social problems. List as many such problems as you can think of. Compare your list with other students. Discuss what other kinds of explanations might account for the social problems you have listed.

COMMON ASSUMPTIONS

It is not only in the media that such images arise. Sociologists, too, have often adopted heterosexual and ethnocentric assumptions in their studies of families, ignoring difference and diversity, and focussing instead on dominant stereotypes. Until quite recently, the study of lesbian and gay families, and ethnic minority families was confined to the margins of mainstream sociological research. This situation is now changing, largely under the influence of the work of feminist scholars who, as we have seen, challenged both traditional notions of family as well as orthodox social scientific approaches towards it. But, acknowledging one's own implicit assumptions requires a level of self–reflection (or 'reflexivity') that is not always easy to achieve, particularly in the light of the persistent tendency in social science to value objective rather than subjective accounts, and the premium placed upon the search for easily generalised, rather than situational or contingent knowledge. Despite this, however, some sociologists have produced valuable information about family forms that do not correspond to white or heterosexual norms.

Activity

Consult recent issues of *Social Trends* or the *Office for National Statistics* publications to find out what proportion of households currently conform to the nuclear family stereotype.

DIVERSITIES WITHIN AND AMONG DIFFERENT FAMILY FORMS

It is also worth pointing out that there exists great diversity among even nuclear family structures. For example, in some, both parents go out to work, and children are cared for by others — relatives, friends, employees. It is usually mothers, or other women, who care for children on a day–to–day basis, but this is not always the case, and there are some families where the father has taken over this role. An increasing number of families are 'reconstituted' families, where one or both parents has been previously divorced or may have brought with them children from a previous relationship. The point being made here is that the nuclear family itself is not a single entity, and that a diversity of family forms can be found within that broad category.

Activity

Not all nuclear families are the same. Consider the ways in which they can differ from each other, and make a list of the dimensions of difference. Do the same for gay and lesbian families.

GAY AND LESBIAN FAMILIES

Same sex desires and behaviour have undoubtedly long existed in most, if not all, human societies. Yet the emergence of the category of 'gay and lesbian families' is historically a very recent occurrence. As such, it is still the subject of much heated debate, and most people have an opinion about it. When quite recently, a gay Scottish couple were approved as adoptive parents, the media felt this was something we should all be told about. Similarly, when one woman in a lesbian couple gave birth to a baby boy as a result of donor insemination, the event provided headline copy for the tabloids. Subsequently, when the women's relationship ended, the tabloids could hardly contain their glee, and used the opportunity to re–visit the old themes about the desirability of heterosexual marriage, to decry the 'unnaturalness' of same sex relationships, and to portray such families as doomed to failure, with adverse consequences for all concerned, particularly the children.

Gay and lesbian families clearly threaten heterosexual ideals about what families should be. They push at the boundaries of social acceptability, and are apt to provoke a range of reactions from outright condemnation, through vague tolerance, to idealisation; it is difficult to feel neutral about such emotive issues. These issues are emotive ones because they go to the heart of the institutionalised heterosexuality, reflected in marriage, upon which our society's ideas about what families are, are based.

SOCIAL SCIENTIFIC EVIDENCE

However, there is growing evidence that the sexual orientation of parents matters very little, if at all, to children's development. Most researchers would now agree that it is not the gender or sexual orientation of parents that matters, but the love, security, support and care that they give the child, and the overall quality of the parenting that they can provide. It was once thought that growing up in a gay or lesbian family would somehow distort a child's own sex–role development and gender identity. On this basis, many lesbian mothers have lost custody of their children, and many gay fathers have had difficulty in maintaining relationships with their children after divorce. Until very recently, judges and courts took a dim view of parents who were open about their homosexuality, but there are now signs that this is beginning to change, and research studies that support the idea that gay and lesbian parents can be every bit as responsible, nurturing, loving, and as effective in their parenting as heterosexual parents, have been produced. A recent review of the research concluded that studies had failed to find any evidence that children of lesbian or gay parents are harmed or compromised or even differ from, in significant ways, children raised in heterosexual families.

Some sociological studies have even begun to suggest that there may be a number of advantages to growing up in a lesbian or gay family. For example, recent British work suggests that children of lesbian co–parents are likely to spend more time and have better quality time with their parents, as the household is less likely to be organised hierarchically, and the women are more likely than their heterosexual counterparts to share tasks equally of wage earning, homemaking and caring for children. Sociologists broadly agree that lesbians tend to have the most egalitarian relationships, and married heterosexual couples the least. Lesbian and gay couples share household chores more equally and with less conflict than do married couples. Other British research, that followed children in lesbian households from childhood to adulthood, found that the young women raised in lesbian households had better relationships with their mothers' lesbian partners than had similar young adults with heterosexual mothers' male partners. These are the sorts of findings that are emerging from recent social scientific research, and they go some way towards redressing the balance and the stigma that has so long been attached to homosexual families.

Study point
Might there be some benefits in growing up in a gay family?

GAY RIGHTS

In some countries, gay and lesbian people are actively struggling to obtain equal family rights with heterosexuals. For instance, some groups have argued for legal recognition of 'gay marriage'; in 1989 Denmark became the first country to permit the legalisation of gay partnerships, and Norway, Sweden and Iceland have since followed suit. In these countries, it is possible to 'register' a partnership (including, incidentally, heterosexual cohabitation) which permits its recognition in law, providing a legal basis for family relationships.

Points of Evaluation

1 Like heterosexual families, it is not possible to define a single category of homosexual families in such a way that would successfully distinguish them from others. Any attempt to do this would first be faced with the problem of what counts as a gay or lesbian family.

2 There are many gay and lesbian people who live with their spouses and cohabitees in arrangements that look remarkably like nuclear families from the outside. In such families, the homosexual parent may or may not have 'come out' to either family or the outside world. On the other hand, there are many same sex couples living with children openly as gay or lesbian parents, and many gay men and lesbian women living alone but with some responsibility for children from previous relationships.

3 Gay and lesbian families come in many guises across society, not confined to any one class or ethnic group; they are as diverse as those we designate as

heterosexual. Moreover, they are likely to do all the same things as other families; going out to work, doing the shopping, cooking, cleaning and laundry, taking the children to the park and helping them with their homework.

4 If gay and lesbian families were socially accepted as legitimate and valid family forms, there would probably be no need for sociologists to talk about 'gay and lesbian families'. However, the continuing struggle by gays and lesbians for recognition of their partnerships and of their parental rights, and for the rights of their children not to be stigmatised, bears testimony to the fact that this day of *normalisation* is yet some way off.

5 Each family is, in a sense, unique, and it is at least as important to attend as much to the differences among gay and lesbian families as to the ways in which they differ from heterosexual families.

6 As we will discuss in chapter 7, the development of new reproductive technologies has made it possible for many people to have children, for whom becoming a parent would previously have been difficult or impossible. The increasing use of such technologies and the increasing social acceptance of surrogacy is permitting gay and lesbian people to have their own genetically–related children.

7 These broader scientific, technological and cultural developments are already having a profound effect on the variety of family forms, and seem likely to lead to an increased visibility and social acceptance of gay and lesbian families.

ETHNIC DIVERSITY

In a multicultural society such as Britain, it is important to consider the ways in which family patterns and structures may vary by ethnic group. However, focussing on diversity raises a number of difficult issues. For example, it may be as misleading to talk about *the* British Asian, or *the* Black Caribbean family as it is to talk about *the* family, since there will be diversity within ethnic family types as well as between them. There is also the danger of lapsing into stereotyping when seeking to describe or explain the patterns and practices of different ethnic groups. There will be some differences and some commonalities across groups in a society, and any definable patterns or tendencies are likely to have both historical antecedents as well as correlates in the present. In Britain, for instance, many people from minority ethnic groups are subjected to outright racism or more subtle forms of discrimination which affects their experiences both inside and outside the family. There is also the issue of mixed race families, of which there are an increasing number in Britain; categorising families by ethnic grouping can be seen as clearly deficient when these families are taken into account.

Nevertheless, sociologists think that it is important to try to describe and explain family patterns and structures across a range of ethnic groups; such an enterprise is necessary if sociology is to reflect the totality of the society we live in, and not just small, dominant sections within it. We actually know remarkably little about families that differ from the white, middle–class, nuclear norm, and the sociological study of families in minority ethnic communities at least goes some way towards addressing this deficiency in sociological knowledge. In this section of the chapter we consider issues of 'race', ethnicity and racism in relation to family life.

DOMINANT TRENDS

Even whilst it is necessary to appreciate the diversity of family forms, and that particular patterns of family life do not straightforwardly map onto particular ethnic groups, official statistics do indicate that there are some identifiable variations in family arrangements adopted by different ethnic groups. For example, Black Caribbean families are more likely to live in lone–parent households than White British and British Asian families. The latter are most likely to live in extended families and to have strong kinship ties. White British and British Asian people are least likely to be single, and Black Caribbean people more likely to be single. These differences may be explained, in part, by the age structures of the groups, but they probably also reflect cultural preferences that derive from social and historical influences on family forms adopted by people of a given cultural heritage. Families where the only continuously present adult is a woman are most common among people of Black Caribbean and African heritage, and least common among people of Asian heritage.

Where these kind of distinctive patterns emerge, it is useful to consider the origins of these differences in history and culture. Sociologists recognise three main influences on family structures:

- Economic influences
- Cultural influences (including language and religion)
- Discrimination and disadvantage

Study point
Consider what might be the effects of racism on families in minority ethnic groups.

BLACK CARIBBEAN FAMILIES

Broadly speaking, three types of family structures have co–existed in the Caribbean, and these have influenced the family patterns of people who emigrated to Britain and their descendants:

- Nuclear families, based on the Christian tradition, found among families who adopted Western values under the influence of colonialism. These families are sometimes referred to as *patriarchal*, or father–headed.
- Long-term co–habitation relationships, not formalised by marriage.
- Mother–headed households, where a woman (a mother or grandmother) is the continuously present adult. These families are sometimes referred to as *matriarchal*.

Historical perspective

Sociologists commonly cite the past history of colonialism and slavery as influential in the development of these family forms. Slavery weakened the bonds between men and women and brought with it prolonged absences of men from the home. Many men were simply unable to support women and children by their own efforts and, for this reason, it is usually only among the wealthier sections of society that families in the Christian tradition are found. The practice of slavery therefore undoubtedly influenced the formation of woman–headed households, as well as the tradition of a network of women helping to look after children whilst other women worked for pay. When working–class Black Caribbean families emigrated to Britain in the late 1940s and 50s, responding to a need to increase the British labour force, established support networks must have been disrupted and traditional sources of help from community and kin would no longer have been available. Many of these families would have faced poverty on arrival in Britain, since wages were lower and living costs were higher than would have been expected, and child care would, in most cases, have had to be paid for. The lack of stable employment, as in slavery, would also have encouraged the persistence of woman–headed households. Yet, women on their own, and those deserted by their partners, with children, would have found it harder to work outside the home, and some were undoubtedly forced into dependence on state benefits, a far cry from the hopes of prosperity in Britain that colonialism encouraged.

Ideologies

In popular political rhetoric, it has been common to adopt a Euro–centrist perspective and to portray the women–dominated families of Black Caribbean communities as a deviation from, or even a rejection of, the so–called traditional family. Such sentiments may have their place in political rhetoric and in the tabloid newspapers, but sociologists prefer to try to understand the historical and cultural influences on different family forms without making judgements about what is desirable and what is not. It is also possible to highlight the positive aspects of difference and to celebrate the contribution made by different family forms to the richness of British culture.

With the second wave of feminism in the 1960s, traditional families came under attack from many prominent feminists as the prime locus for women's oppression. However, as Black women's groups were quick to point out, Black families were different, and the same ideas and theories about family life could not be indiscriminately applied without any reference to history, culture and current conditions. In particular, racism affected and continues to affect people who are identifiably different from the white majority. In this context, the Black family perhaps plays a particularly significant role in providing a safe haven from the ravages of racism that Black people experience in a White–dominated society. Only when Britain becomes a truly multi–cultural society that is prepared to respect difference and to acknowledge its contribution to the richness of British culture, will this particular role for Black families no longer be necessary.

Study point
List the features that sociologists have identified as common among families of Caribbean heritage.

ASIAN FAMILIES

As we have mentioned, there are aspects of British Asian family patterns and structures that exist in direct contrast to those of families in the Black Caribbean and white British communities. However, it has to be said at the outset that 'Asian families' do not comprise a single, uniform grouping. On the contrary, they may be distinguished from each other along lines of religion (for example, Muslim, Sikh, Hindu), country or region of origin, caste, class and language. Nevertheless, sociologists have identified some common patterns. Two features stand out as particularly important in this respect:

• The continuing significance of family and kinship ties. Many British Asian families either live in extended family households, or are in close touch with kin, including kin who have remained in the country of origin. The influence of 'elders' remains, in many cases, very strong.

• The value placed upon marriage. Marriage remains commonplace in British Asian communities as the basis for family life.

Distinctive Patterns

South Asian families tend to be hierarchical and patriarchal, with the husband/father, the undisputed head of the household, controlling the family finances and making the major decisions, albeit in consultation with others. Conjugal roles remain segregated along gender lines. Sociologists have identified the 'typical' basic South Asian family unit as consisting of a man, his sons and his grandsons, together with their wives and their unmarried daughters; at marriage, the daughters become part of the husband's family group. Families tend to live together, or very close to each other, and to work together. Family membership involves a strong sense of duty and obligation to kin, which are hierarchically organised. For example, for a woman or child to challenge a husband's or father's authority in public would be to shame his honour and that of the family as a whole. Arranged marriages between kin groups are still common.

Historical Perspective

When people from India, Pakistan and Bangladesh emigrated to Britain, they arrived in a society very different from their own. For example, many would have found their ideas about honour and family loyalty completely lacking in Britain; the British environment created many challenges to the traditional way of life. Yet, many have managed to maintain these cultural values against all the odds; for some, cultural values have intensified in the face of cultural opposition. Witness, for example, the popularity of fundamentalisms in some Asian groups. The experiences of people who emigrated here are also divided along gender lines. Owing to the male–dominated nature of the culture, many women would have found themselves cut off from the wider society, with both social and language barriers keeping them confined to the home. It is custom in some Muslim and Hindu communities to keep women in seclusion, with clothing that conceals their bodies almost completely when they go out. This custom is commonly referred to as *purdah*.

Sociological Studies

Sociologists have mostly studied second–generation British Asians, those born in Britain who constitute more than half of the Asian community. Studies have documented the conflicts and tensions in the lives of young people from families of Asian heritage who are exposed to two very different cultural influences. Many of the values espoused by mainstream British society, (for example, individuality and autonomy), are in marked contrast to the values British Asian families seek to socialise into their young (for example, co–operation, family loyalty, respect for elders, and obedience). Young people in Britain are judged largely on the merits of what they, as individuals, achieve, not on their membership of a particular group. They are exposed to a rapidly changing 'youth culture' whose values directly and necessarily conflict with those of the older generation, and which thrives on pushing the boundaries of authority.

Many young people in British Asian communities have risen creatively to the challenge presented by such conflicts and tensions. These people, perhaps, are steering a way towards becoming truly multi–cultural, forging their identities in positive ways that take account of both family demands and the need to fit in to a wider cultural framework. Many do this by adapting their behaviour as situations and circumstances warrant, recognising both the value to them of close family relationships and support, as well as individual autonomy and achievement in the wider world outside the family. Even arranged marriages, that so conflict with the dominant Western ideal of romantic love, can be creatively tolerated, or even welcomed. And it is interesting to note that recent social scientific research is beginning to produce some evidence that such marriages are as likely to 'work' in the longer term as any other.

Study point

List the features that sociologists have identified as common among families of Asian heritage.

Points of Evaluation

1   It is not possible to state unequivocally that certain family formations easily map onto particular ethnic groups, despite the popular appeal of such a sentiment. On the contrary, differences within communities are large and may be more or less pronounced by generation.
2   Undoubtedly, socio-economic differences are a factor, affecting the influences that Western culture has on family life. For example the Bangladeshi people, who were among the first Asians to settle in Britain, took up largely unskilled jobs; the women were expected to marry young and to have children. This has probably affected the rate of teenage pregnancy in the community, which is relatively high.

SUMMARY POINTS

1   Difference and diversity in family structures and patterns abound in contemporary British society, bearing testimony to the fact that it is impossible to identify a unitary construction of *the* family.
2   Families that deviate from the heterosexual, white, married nuclear 'norm' may be denigrated in the press, and blamed for a host of social ills in political rhetoric, but in the eyes and minds of individuals, they constitute families nevertheless. Were it not for political and ideological imperatives, these families would take their place alongside others as ordinary British families.

SUMMARY

Many families in Britain depart from the ideal of the white, heterosexual, nuclear norm, and instead exhibit a bewildering diversity in forms and patterns. Real families, even those that appear 'traditional', raise the spectre of difference and remind us that a unitary concept of the family is inadequate to capture diverse realities. Families that depart from the desired ideal are often unsupported at best and, at worst, are sometimes blamed for a host of social ills, from educational under–achievement to juvenile crime. The rhetoric is a powerful one, and is reproduced daily in the tabloid press.

Gay and lesbian families threaten the heterosexual ideal of what families *should* be, and provoke emotive debates. Yet the existing evidence suggests that children are not harmed, and may even benefit in some ways, from growing up in such households. Some countries have recognised this, and have passed laws that enable homosexual couples to formalise and legalise their relationships. This has not yet happened in Britain. If gay and lesbian families were socially accepted as legitimate family forms, there would be no need for sociologists to study them as special categories.

Britain is a multicultural society, but the problem of racism has not yet been conquered. As families are intimately linked to society, one would expect family forms and patterns to vary according to cultural heritage. To some extent, they do. By and large, Black Caribbean families are identifiably different from British Asian families and British White families, but sociologists recognise that it is important not to focus just on difference, at the expense of things all families have in common, and at the expense of diversity within ethnic groups. It is also important not to lapse into stereotyping when talking about differences. The differences that can be observed may be explained with reference to cultural heritages, including class, religion and current circumstances.

STUDY GUIDES

Group activities

1 In your group, search through recent issues of *Social Trends*, *Population Trends* and the *Office for National Statistics* publications to find out about the statistical evidence for family patterns in minority ethnic communities. Make a table of your findings.

2 Consult recent reports of the *British Social Attitudes Survey* to find out what people think about lone–parents. Devise a short questionnaire and use it to do some research of your own into this issue. How do your findings compare with the published data?

3 Conduct a class debate: 'Homosexual partnerships should be legally recognised'.

4 The issue of trans–racial adoption, particularly the adoption of Black children by White families, continues to cause debate. Discuss the benefits and disadvantages of these arrangements, ensuring that you think about the issues from the perspectives of *both* the birth family *and* the adoptive parents.

Practice questions

Item A

The data under review suggest that the gender and family structures of ethnic minority groups are subject to change and continuity. They show that in Afro–Caribbean communities, extended family relationships are weaker than they were in the Caribbean, that the grandmother family is virtually non–existent and that there may be tendencies to higher rates of marriage and more symmetrical conjugal role relationships. Nevertheless, Afro–Caribbean family patterns remain distinctive in terms of the institutional weakness of marriage, the prevalence of woman–headed families, the marginality of men and the orientation of women towards economic independence ...

In Asian communities, extra-nuclear family loyalties are less extensive, women are more often in the labour force, the arranged marriage is becoming more flexible and married relationships are in general closer than was customary in rural South Asia in the 1950s and 1960s. However, the evidence suggests that Asian ideals of family loyalty and obligation, of the primacy of mothering in women's lives and of male authority are being reproduced. The low rates of unmarried cohabitation, divorce and solo parenthood among Asian peoples ... together with their low rate of inter-marriage with people of other ethnicities ... are evidence of the continuing integrity of Asian family values.

In sum, it appears that the gender and family structures of Afro–Caribbean and Asian groups have changed in the context of cultural, economic and political opportunities and constraints of life in Britain but in ways that are shaped by their own cultural logic.

Faith Robertson Elliott, 1996, *Gender, Family and Society*, Macmillan, p57.

---

1 With reference to Item A and elsewhere, list the main defining features of Afro–Caribbean (Black Caribbean) households.

2 With reference to Item A and elsewhere, list the main defining features of British Asian households.

3 With reference to elsewhere, discuss three explanations that have been offered to account for the distinctive features of Afro–Caribbean families.

4 Critically evaluate the idea that Afro–Caribbean family patterns reflect the legacy of slavery.

5 With reference to Item A and elsewhere, discuss the main dimensions of (a) change and (b) continuity in the family patterns commonly observed in British Asian communities.

6 With reference to elsewhere, assess the contribution made by women of colour to the feminist critique of the family.

Coursework suggestions

1 Describe how family structures, patterns and values vary according to ethnic heritage, and explain how this diversity may be accounted for.

2 Defend or attack the proposition that 'The domestic division of labour in lesbian households provides an egalitarian model that could usefully be imitated in heterosexual families'.

6

INTIMACY, COHABITATION, MARRIAGE AND DIVORCE

Introduction

THERE CAN BE no doubt that the meanings of intimacy, and the associated patterns of domestic arrangements, and family forms, are undergoing change in our society. We have already discussed the ways in which such changes have given rise to concerns about social stability and the future of 'the family'. The high divorce rate, the increasing numbers of births outside of marriage and the declining marriage rate, however, are but aspects of broader social changes that both derive from and affect changing family practices, values, beliefs and attitudes. Sociologists have been in the forefront among those who document and debate the complexities of these issues, issues that are of immediate relevance to the understanding of our society as a whole, and to social policy responses that lay frameworks for the future organisation and management of our domestic lives. In this chapter, we consider the complex nature of what sociologist Anthony Giddens refers to as the contemporary 'transformation of intimacy', and other sociological work that illuminates the personal meanings and impact of such a transformation. Opinion is divided over the issue of whether contemporary changes in family life represent a positive step forward, towards acceptance of difference and diversity, or a damaging retreat from traditional values.

Table 6: *Key concepts and issues*	
KEY CONCEPTS	KEY ISSUES
Intimacy Transformation of intimacy Cohabitation Marriage Marriage rate Divorce Divorce rate Serial monogamy	What are the features that characterise 'late modernity'? What is 'serial monogamy'? Why, according to Giddens, are the *meanings* of intimacy changing? What significance do changes in gender roles have in this development? Why are sex and reproduction no longer as firmly linked together as they were a couple of generations ago? Are contemporary intimate relationships really purely a matter of personal choice? How important are blood ties? How frequent are births outside marriage? What are the effects of divorce on children?

INTIMACY

Giddens argues that, in contemporary Western industrialised societies, we are moving inexorably away from the values and certainties of 'modernity', and instead inhabit a new terrain where novel values and mentalities, currently only emerging, will dominate to fashion our lives. Some sociologists refer to contemporary times as the 'post–modern' age; others (Giddens among them) prefer to talk about 'late modernity'. Whatever label is attached, most agree that fast disappearing are the old forms of left/right politics and the boundaries of 'nation' that confined us. Science, that quintessential bastion of certainty and progress in the 'modern' period, from the Enlightenment onwards, is increasingly challenged; knowledge is fragmenting, and is increasingly recognised as situationally produced, as the grand meta–narratives of modernity give way to the local, contingent narratives of our own times. Old certainties, shared moralities and consensus values are all being transformed under the impact of global economic and technological change, that carries us along in its wake. Giddens is, of course, talking about social change from the point of view of Western industrialised societies, although obviously the changes we witness in the industrialised world will also have an effect upon 'developing' nations. Part and parcel of these changes are changes in intimacy, which Giddens sees as impacting on our views, expectations and experiences of family life.

A major transformation in the meaning of intimacy is underway, and this is closely linked with, on the one hand, what we do in families and, on the other hand, what we expect and desire families to do for us. Giddens argues that our closest intimate relationships, once founded on romantic love, are becoming more pragmatic and contingent. Mentalities are changing, so that we no longer look for Mr or Mrs Right, but rather we search for the perfect relationship; when one fails to satisfy, the individual in late modernity increasingly feels free to move on to try another. Romantic love, as a basis for intimate partnerships, Giddens argues is being replaced by what he calls 'confluent' love as the basis for the 'pure' relationship, as marriage for life, 'till death us do part' is replaced by *serial monogamy*. Giddens sees these changing mentalities around intimacy as underlying the propensity for divorce in industrialised Western societies.

Study point
List the features that characterise 'romantic' love. How does Giddens' concept of 'confluent' love differ?

What is at stake here are the changing *meanings* of intimate relationships. In the 1950s, for example, surveys showed that the most important aspect of marriage was the fulfilling of gender–differentiated, breadwinner–homemaker, roles. By the 1970s, similar surveys showed the most important thing to be that husbands and wives liked each other. In the intervening years, there was a change in emphasis from the *structure* of the relationship to its *quality*. Nevertheless, as the most recent social attitudes surveys show, monogamy and fidelity remain important values shared by the great majority of people.

MARRIAGE AND COHABITATION

Over the last twenty years in Britain, the marriage rate has halved. In 1971, it was 68 per thousand, but by 1991 this had fallen to 36 per thousand. Over the same period, remarriages for one or both partners increased from 20% to 36%, though more recently, the remarriage rate has begun to fall. Yet Britain still has one of the highest marriage rates in Europe. Sociologists have identified a range of factors that work together and help to explain the decline in the numbers of people getting married. These include:

- More people are delaying marriage (and parenthood) until later in life
- Greater acceptance of cohabitation (either as a substitute for, or as a prelude to marriage)
- Greater acceptance of sex and parenthood outside of marriage, and the consequent separation of marriage, sex and reproduction
- Increasing numbers of women who are economically active outside the home and capable of financial independence
- Influence of high divorce rates
- Transformations in the meanings and values of intimacy

TRADITIONAL MARRIAGE

Sociologists have identified a number of dimensions along which 'traditional' marriages differ from contemporary intimate partnerships. Traditional marriage was first and foremost a social institution, with clearly defined roles and associated norms, based on gender and age segregation. Men were primarily 'breadwinners', responsible for bringing home a 'family wage' to support wife and children, and women were primarily 'housewives', responsible for homemaking, child rearing and care of the sick and elderly in the home. Marriage brought with it social and kinship ties, and implied certain expectations and obligations to others. Sexuality and reproduction were firmly linked together in marriage. Sex before marriage was socially unacceptable (although it was undoubtedly quite common), and pre–marital pregnancy often resulted in 'shot–gun weddings' or the adoption, by a married couple, of the resulting infant. Marriage was for life, and divorce was stigmatised. Marriage, by definition, was heterosexual, and provided the model for all intimate partnerships.

Activity
Refer to official statistics and find out what has happened to the marriage rate over the last 50 years.

NEW FORMS OF INTIMATE RELATIONSHIPS

By contrast, contemporary forms of intimate partnerships are transforming some, or all, of these traditional dimensions of marriage. Partnerships have become much more a matter of personal choice. The most important dimension of contemporary partnerships is their relational (interpersonal and emotional) aspect; partners expect equality, sharing and companionship, and they expect satisfaction and self–fulfilment from their relationships. Roles no longer straightforwardly imply duties; rather, as Janet Finch's work has shown, obligations to kin are fulfilled only to the extent that one chooses to fulfil them. Sexuality is seen as something we all have a right to enjoy, including in same sex partnerships. Having or not having children is also a matter of personal choice; we no longer need a long–term partner, or even a partner, to become a parent, and the former links between sex, marriage and reproduction have been broken. Increasing numbers of people cohabit, whether as a prelude to, or as a substitute for, marriage. There is still a premium placed on fidelity, however, such that serial monogamy has replaced marriage–for–life as the norm.

Study point
How do contemporary intimate partnerships differ from traditional marriages? In what ways are they the same?

EXPLAINING CONTEMPORARY PATTERNS

In chapter 1 we discussed the difficulties in defining the term 'family' in the light of historically changing family patterns, and contemporary cultural diversity, and we saw how these changes were reflected in demographic statistics and in attitude surveys. In this chapter, we have been looking at the changing meanings of intimate relationships; the meaning of marriage is now very different from what it was in our parents' and grandparents' generations, and a diverse variety of partnerships have become increasingly popular as the marriage rate has fallen. Divorce has also become more commonplace. Legislation over the course of this century has made divorce more accessible and available to a wider range of people. For example, the 1949 Legal Aid Act made public funds available to assist with the cost of divorce for poorer families. External supports for marriage, such as those associated with religion and community, have diminished in some, though not all, sections of society. Church–going among the Christian population is much less popular than it was fifty years ago, but traditional religion retains its significance for many Muslim families.

At the same time, sociologists also point out that the pressures on marriage have increased. Many families are now dual–earner families, with both men and women going out to work. Yet the advent of domestic technologies and consumer products has had the effect of increasing the burdens of housework, as higher standards for food preparation and household hygiene are now demanded. In addition, raising children now includes a significant educational element, increasing the tasks that parents are expected to do. Hochschild captures this increased burden in her idea about the 'double shift' that women do.

Activity

List the factors that sociologists invoke to explain the declining marriage rate.

A range of influences have combined to destabilise the sex–marriage–reproduction linkage of earlier times, and some sociologists now argue that parenthood has replaced marriage as the basis for family life. Some also suggest that, in future, marriage is likely to be replaced by new forms of commitment, such as parenting agreements or private contractual arrangements. For example, the law now permits unmarried parents to enter into 'parental responsibility' agreements that are legally binding; and unmarried fathers can obtain court orders for 'parental responsibility' even where the mother does not agree. In future 'blood ties' could begin to lose their significance, especially with the advent of new reproductive technologies. There are likely to be increasing numbers of families where biological ties are absent, and where kinship networks are based instead on choice and affinity rather than blood. For example, the law permits lesbian co–parents to apply for orders in respect of children who are not biologically related to them and where the tie is only a social one.

CHILDBEARING OUTSIDE MARRIAGE

Nearly 60% of couples who marry will have lived together (cohabited) first. Approximately one third of babies are born outside of marriage, many of them to cohabiting parents. The increase over the last two decades in unmarried cohabitation and extra–marital childbearing has been seen as perhaps the most dramatic dimension of recent changes in family life. Cohabitation differs from marriage in a number of ways. Most cohabitations are short–lived, lasting an average of two to three years before the partners either separate or marry (the average marriage lasts in the region of ten years). Cohabitation relationships seem to be less stable than marriage, although this is difficult to estimate. Sociologists have suggested that cohabitation is best regarded as a stage of courtship, rather than as a substitute for marriage, since many cohabiting couples go on to marry.

Activity

Consider how cohabitation differs from marriage. Compare ideas with other students in your group.

The frequency of births outside marriage was taken by commentators in Victorian times as an important indicator of the moral state of the nation, with high rates giving rise to fears about social dysfunction and moral decline. We can see the legacy of these ideas reflected in our own times, in contemporary concerns about lone–mothers and teenage pregnancies. Yet nowadays the stigma attached to childbearing outside marriage is less marked than it was even in the 1960s. With the legalisation of abortion in 1967, and the advent of the contraceptive pill, births outside of marriage are more likely than they were to be a matter of positive choice than bad luck.

Since the beginning of the 1980s, births outside marriage have tripled. Approximately a third of babies are born to unmarried parents, although the majority (about three quarters) are registered jointly by both parents, many of whom give the same address and are therefore likely to be cohabiting.

Never–married women living alone with children are amongst the poorest people in our society. The vast majority live in rented accommodation, typically provided by the local authority and paid for by housing benefit. The majority receive Income Support and only a small minority are in paid employment. Most are aged between 20 and 34 years, and are likely to have few, if any, educational qualifications. These young women are caught in what is commonly referred to as the 'poverty trap', unable to earn a living wage because of a lack of qualifications and of affordable child care. Successive governments in Britain have expressed concern about the consequences for the children growing up in such families; it is not uncommon to hear the lives of these families associated with crime, immorality and delinquency, yet little practical help (such as free child care) has been forthcoming. It is difficult to escape the conclusion that such families provide convenient 'scapegoats'; they deviate from the desired two–parent, heterosexual norm and are blamed for a range of social problems. Sociologists would argue that the denigration, common in the media, of such families is one instance of the operation of an ideology that seeks to support the nuclear family and the 'sanctity of marriage'.

DIVORCE

In our century, the divorce statistics have been a major cause for concern; divorce has been seen as *the* social problem of our age. Particularly since the Second World War, there has been an increase in divorce of quite dramatic proportions. Some commentators have concluded that the high divorce rate, accompanied by the decline in the popularity of marriage, signifies nothing less than a contemporary 'crisis in the family', heralding a demise in 'family values' that threatens the whole basis of social order. Others take a different view, and argue that contemporary divorce rates tells us little, if anything, about the state of

Table 7: *Marriages and Divorces over the last century: numbers and rates**				
YEAR	MARRIAGES (TOTAL NUMBERS)	DIVORCES (TOTAL NUMBERS)	MARRIAGE (**SEE BELOW)	DIVORCE (***SEE BELOW)
1899	262,344	468	16.5	not available
1900	257,480	512	16.0	not available
1910	267,721	596	15.0	not available
1920	379,982	3,090	20.2	not available
1930	315,109	3,563	15.8	not available
1940	470,549	7,755	22.5	not available
1945	397,626	15,634	18.7	not available
1950	358,490	30,870	16.3	2.8
1955	357,918	26,816	16.1	2.4
1960	343,614	23,868	15.0	2.0
1965	371,127	37,783	15.6	3.1
1970	415,487	58,239	17.0	4.7
1975	380,620	120,522	15.4	9.6
1980	370,022	148,301	14.9	12.0
1983	344,334	147,479	13.9	12.2
1986	347,924	153,903	13.9	12.9
1987	351,761	151,007	14.0	12.7
1988	348,492	152,633	13.8	12.8
1989	346,697	150,872	13.7	12.7
1990	331,150	153,386	13.1	13.0
1991	306,756	158,745	12.0	13.4
1992	311,564	160,385	12.2	13.7
1993	299,197	165,018	11.6	14.2
1994	291,069	158,175	11.3	13.7
1995	283,012	155,499	10.9	13.6
1996	278,975	157,107	10.7	13.8

*TABLE COMPILED WITH STATISTICS TAKEN FROM MARRIAGE AND DIVORCE STATISTICS, 1837–1983, OFFICE FOR NATIONAL STATISTICS, MARRIAGES SUMMARY SERIES FM2, NO.16 AND MARRIAGE AND DIVORCE STATISTICS, OFFICE FOR NATIONAL STATISTICS, DIVORCES SERIES FM2, NO.24

**MARRIAGE RATE: PERSONS MARRYING PER 1000 POPULATION OF ALL AGES

***DIVORCE RATE: RATES PER 1000 MARRIED POPULATION

marriage or of society as a whole. Sociologists remain divided on the question of the significance of high divorce rates and falling marriage rates in contemporary society. Some argue that divorce rates alert us to a range of pressures and strains that beset marriage in our society, and that married life often fails to live up to the high expectations that we have of it. (See Table 7.)

There are complex issues involved here. In chapter 1 we discussed the changing demographic patterns of family life that illustrate a contemporary diversity of family arrangements, such that the ideal nuclear family currently represents only a small proportion of household forms. On the other hand, we saw that sociological work on attitudes towards and beliefs about family life demonstrates some persistence of traditional values, although these are less marked amongst younger people. These conflicting kinds of sociological evidence have led sociologists to recognise that there is a gap between what people do in families and what they believe ideally should be done. Sociologists are able to reconcile the conflicting evidence by thinking about the changing *meanings* of family and marriage; as history proceeds and society evolves, each generation has rather different ideas than the previous one about what intimacy involves, and about what marriage implies and about what divorce represents.

Divorce no longer carries the stigma or the connotations of failure that it did when our grandparents were young. On the contrary, changes in the law have made divorce easier, more accessible to greater numbers and more socially acceptable as a way out of an unhappy (or even abusive) relationship. On the other hand, the ideology of marriage and of the 'intact' nuclear family has persisted in many ways, and it is true to say that there continues to exist a profound tension, a contradiction even, between romantic ideals that underlie marriage and the likelihood of divorce.

In the early 1990s there was one divorce for every two new marriages. But sociologists recognise that divorce rates do not simply reflect the numbers of unsatisfactory marriages; legal changes, too, have their impact. The doubling of the numbers of divorces in the early 1970s, for example, was more a consequence of changes in the law in 1969 (which altered the grounds for divorce), than a reflection of any real increase in the numbers of people who wanted to end unhappy marriages. Since then, the overall rise in divorces has been much more gradual. The peak reached in the mid–1980s again is probably a statistical 'blip' that reflects a further legislative change in 1984 which permitted divorce petitions to be filed after only one year of marriage. The divorce rate, therefore, does not simply reflect changing familial attitudes and values and, on its own, cannot be counted as good sociological evidence of social change.

Study point
Does legislation have an effect on the divorce rate?

Nevertheless, it is important to recognise that, as time goes by, divorces have been occurring with increasing frequency, and increasingly earlier on in marriage. Of marriages that took place in 1951, for example, some 10% ended in divorce within 25 years; but among couples who married in 1971, 10% had divorced by their 6th anniversary, and of those married in 1981, 10% had divorced before five years had passed. Current estimates are that two to three out of five marriages are likely to end in divorce. The sociological evidence can be worrying for those who support the 'traditional' family, based around marriage. The worrying factors may be summarised as follows:

- Marriages do not last as long as they used to; most divorces occur between 5-9 years after marriage, so marriage is no longer 'for life'.
- More than 70% of divorce petitions are filed by women, and most of these are based on allegations of 'unreasonable behaviour', often including violence and abuse.
- There are a number of 'risk factors' for divorce that sociologists have identified. These include marrying under age 21, having divorced parents, having lived together before marriage, and second or subsequent marriage. It is important to note, however, that these risk factors are statistically–derived, and do not constitute 'causes' for marital breakdown.
- Britain has one of the highest divorce rates in Europe, but it also has one of the highest marriage rates.
- More than half of couples who divorce have children under 16 years of age.

Activity

Refer to official statistics and find out how Britain's marriage and divorce rates compare to those of other European countries.

CHILDREN AND DIVORCE

Over the last twenty five years, sociologists (and psychologists) have expressed concern over the growing proportion of children who are affected by parental divorce. Currently, one in four children will experience the divorce of their parents before they reach the age of 16. In popular rhetoric, divorce is widely seen as damaging to children; not only may it result in the disruption or severance of emotional bonds, but it can also lead to a severe decline in living standards and, consequently, life chances. Sociologists have shown that children of divorce are more likely to be living in poverty and to leave school earlier with fewer qualifications, than their counterparts in non-divorced families. In addition, these children often face the challenges associated with their parents' new relationships, the establishment of step–families and the arrival of new siblings. Children of divorced parents may have only intermittent, or no contact with the non–resident parent, usually the father, and may receive little, or no, financial support from him.

Since the 1970s, there has been a large amount of social scientific study into the effects of divorce on children. These studies have tended to look for, and to find, adverse consequences of parental separation, over both the shorter and the longer term. These include emotional difficulties and behavioural problems, educational under–achievement, and impaired life chances. However, studies vary so much in their sampling techniques and their methodologies, that it is difficult to make direct comparisons between them, or indeed to arrive at any general conclusion overall. The outcomes for children seem to depend upon a range of factors, including gender, age, availability of social and economic support, and the quality of the child's relationships with her or his parents. In some circumstances, outcomes can actually be positive, particularly where the divorce marks the end of a violent or otherwise abusive relationship. For some children, divorce represents an opportunity to discover new strengths and to acquire new skills to meet life's challenges. Therefore, whilst divorce is, in most cases, acutely traumatic in the short term, the longer term picture is by no means a bleak one, and it is important not to lose sight of the fact that there can be winners and survivors, as well as losers, in divorce.

Summary of the British Research

In 1998, researchers Bryan Rodgers and Jan Pryor conducted a comprehensive review of the British research into the outcomes for children of divorced parents. The issues covered by the studies, and their findings, are summarised below. However, it is important to remember that different studies have focused on different populations and have yielded different results. Many, although not all, studies have concluded that, overall, divorce has negative consequences for children, both in childhood and adulthood; some commentators are more pessimistic than others. It is important to point out that there is no simple, or direct, relationship between parental separation and children's adjustment, as many factors enter into the equation. As Rodgers and Pryor point out, there is no reason to think, on the basis of the research studies, that all children will suffer as a result of parental separation or divorce.

- *Separated vs intact families: socio–economic circumstances of parents and their children*: There is a strong relationship between poverty and disadvantage in childhood. As many divorced families suffer acute or prolonged economic hardship, the effects of poverty may account for many of the difficulties those children face.
- *Separated vs intact families: socio-economic outcomes for offspring in adulthood*: For many children, the economic disadvantage persists into adulthood, in terms of income level, unemployment and housing.
- *Separated vs intact families: childhood emotional problems and disorders*: Psychological and behavioural distress is common, though more severe psychological disturbance is not. Some studies have indicated that children of separated parents, particularly boys in the two years following separation, are

at an increased risk for conduct disorders. Not much is known about the precise factors that ameliorate or exacerbate that risk, although family conflict, parent–child relationships and other events subsequent to separation are likely to be influential.

- *Separated vs intact families: antisocial behaviour and delinquency in childhood and adulthood*: The association between family structure and anti–social or delinquent/criminal behaviour has been the subject of speculation at least since the 1940s and the influential work of psychologist John Bowlby who proposed a link between the separation of mother and child in early life and disrupted development. Research tends to show higher levels of anti–social behaviour in children of separated families, but there is no consensus regarding the underlying 'causes'.

- *Separated vs intact families: educational attainment*: Children of separated parents tend to show signs of impaired concentration and educational performance. However, many of theses differences disappear when socio-economic factors are taken into account.

- *Separated vs intact families: physical health*: Studies suggest that children from separated families are slightly more at risk of accidents and health problems than their counterparts in intact families, but there are few studies and the findings are mixed.

- *Separated vs intact families: life transitions — age of leaving school, home; sexual behaviour, partnership and parenthood*: Several UK studies suggest that parental separation is associated with an increased likelihood of leaving home and school at an early age, and of early sexual activity, pregnancy and partnership. However, many young people do not enter into this sequence of early transitions, and many factors are likely to contribute to outcomes.

- *Separated vs intact families: mental health and substance use in adolescence and adulthood*: There is a considerable literature on the association between parental separation and mental health in adulthood. For example, adults from separated families are twice as likely to suffer depression as adults from intact families. Parental separation has also been linked to increased rates of smoking and illicit drug use. These findings however do not indicate what underlying factors contribute to the reported relationships, and it is important to bear in mind that the problems are typically evident in only a small minority of children from separated families, and social circumstances are likely to be influential.

In the 1970s when the early large scale studies were published, researchers tended to attribute the adverse effects of divorce to the 'loss' of a parent (usually the father). By the 1980s though, researchers had begun to recognise that the 'loss' model was perhaps over–simplified and had limited explanatory power. They began to recognise the importance of changed economic circumstances for longer term outcomes, and to focus more on the quality of the child's relationships and the kind of support available to children. More recently, the model has been refined further, and it is now recognised that conflict between parents, before, during and after divorce, is one of the most important factors affecting children's development. For this reason, legislation has been passed in a number of countries, including Britain and the United States, that seeks to take the heat out of divorce and to minimise the opportunities for parental conflict. At the same time, ideologies have sought to promote co–operative co–parenting after divorce. However, divorce is a psychologically difficult time for adults too, and no one finds it easy to put their angry feelings aside; as many studies have shown, co–operative co–parenting after divorce remains more an ideal than a reality for most people.

Study point
List the factors that are important in influencing the outcomes for children of divorce.

Legislation

Recent legislative changes have prioritised children's needs and have attempted, often unsuccessfully, to maintain children's relationships with non–resident fathers and to enforce fathers' financial obligations towards their children.

- The Matrimonial and Family Proceedings Act 1984 provided that the 'welfare of the child' should be a 'first consideration' when courts make financial and property orders on divorce.
- The Children Act 1989 was designed to encourage fathers' commitment to and relationships with their children.
- The Child Support Act 1991 obliged fathers to provide a measure of financial support, calculated according to a precise formula, for children whom they had left or, in some cases, never known.

But, the enforcement of these policy objectives has proved to be more problematic, in practice, than was envisaged when the laws were passed by Parliament. For example, many fathers continue to fade out from children's lives within a few years of divorce or separation, and there has been vociferous opposition to the provisions of the child support legislation, such that the Act itself has been subjected to a number of reviews. It is true to say that legislative change seems to have had relatively little impact upon the beliefs and practices of parents. We shall explore this issue further in chapter 7 but, for the moment, it is sufficient to say that there is no one–to–one relationship between the family values espoused by our legislators and those encountered 'on the ground' amongst real people.

Family Ideology

The ideology of the family, based around marriage, as the cornerstone of society and the guarantor of social stability, underlies family law but does not necessarily produce the desired effects. We may regularly be faced with worrying images of the 'damage' done to children by divorce, and the detrimental effects of 'fatherless families' but, nevertheless, couples continue to divorce, an increasing number of children are born to never–married women and fathers regularly renege on the responsibilities society sets out for them.

Sociologists explain this paradoxical state of affairs with reference to prevailing ideas about the meanings of motherhood and fatherhood, which we shall explore in more detail in the next chapter. Suffice to say, at this stage, that motherhood has traditionally been seen as more central to children's development, whilst fatherhood has more often been equated with the provider role. The government of the day may appear to advocate that we abandon these old ideas but, in fact, they continue to be reflected in economic and social policies. For example, employers in Britain do not provide for paid paternity leave, in the same way that they provide for mothers to have time off work when babies are born. Fathers today face obstacles to becoming all–round caring parents that have their origins in both individual psychology and social structures and accepted economic practices whilst mothers, in the main, continue to carry the burdens associated with the raising of children. In this context, it is hardly surprising that arrangements for children on divorce continue to reflect old gendered ideologies and practices, and that our legislators face an uphill struggle in their attempt to make fathers either more nurturing or more financially responsible.

Study point
What image of children underlies concern about their welfare in divorce?

The Children's Perspective

What do children themselves say about their parents' divorce? Somewhat surprisingly, there has been very little social scientific research into this important question. A cursory look at the underlying images of children that have informed both our legislative programme in family law and a good deal of the research on children and divorce, reveals a picture of the child–as–victim, rendered at best vulnerable, and at worst damaged by the experience. This image is a powerful one, and it links closely with a broader image of childhood that exists in our culture.

Sociologists talk about the way in which childhood is 'socially constructed', as a state of being that is less competent and more vulnerable than adulthood, with children consequently requiring the protection of adults or of the State. Sociologists James and Prout argue that this is an 'adultist' perspective that actually undermines children's own human agency, and results in the creation of children as an oppressed group, lacking the kind of basic human rights that adults take for granted. In divorce cases, as well as in research, the dominance of this image of the child as vulnerable, has resulted in an absence of children's own voices; what children themselves think, feel and say has rarely been heard.

Activity
Collect some information about divorce from your local county court and/or your local mediation service. Discuss what you have found with other students.

However, over the last few years, sociological researchers have attempted to tip the balance in favour of children. Studies are beginning to be published that document what children themselves say. What they overwhelmingly say about divorce is that they want their views to be taken account of; they do not want to choose between parents, neither do they want to feel responsible for post–divorce arrangements for their care, but they do want to be involved in the changes that affect their lives, and to have a chance to contribute to the decision–making process.

SUMMARY

According to Giddens, the meanings and practices of intimacy are undergoing change in late modern society. Marriage rates are declining, whilst divorce rates are increasing, more people are cohabiting (either as a prelude to or as a substitute for marriage) and more babies are being born to non–married parents. Gender relations are undergoing change, as women take their place in the labour market. People increasingly expect personal satisfaction and fulfilment from their intimate partnerships. Giddens refers to these contemporary phenomena as the 'transformation of intimacy'. He argues that romantic love, as a basis for intimate partnerships, is being replaced by the more pragmatic and contingent 'confluent' love, and lifelong marriage is being replaced by serial monogamy.

Issues of personal choice are also important in the context of family obligations. People are no longer as bound by a sense of duty as they were in previous generations. The support and care we give to others, for example the elderly, is now more a matter of personal choice than social duty.

The former links among sex, marriage and reproduction are also being severed. Sexuality is seen as something we all have a right to enjoy, inside or outside of marriage, and since the advent of effective contraceptives, sexual relations need only lead to parenthood when we want it to.

Legislation over the past century has made divorce more accessible to a greater number of people, and some of the external religious and community supports for marriage are decreasing in significance. Pressures on marriage have increased, especially for women in dual earner families. Cohabitation relationships seem to be less durable than marriage. Sociologists are divided on the question of whether cohabitation is a new stage in courtship, or whether it is becoming a substitute for marriage.

Policy makers have been concerned about the effects of these changes for society as a whole. Particular concerns have been raised about the effects of divorce on children. These concerns are best understood in the context of powerful ideologies about society's need for stable, intact families. Divorce can be emotionally traumatic, it is disruptive of children's relationships with their parents (and wider kin groups) and often brings severe financial hardship in its wake. Research shows that it can adversely affect children's life chances. The negative images of divorce that pervade our culture reflect the personal and social anxieties divorce produces. However, for some, divorce can be a developmental challenge, a chance to find new strengths and to acquire new skills. Particularly when it means the end of an abusive and destructive relationship, divorce can be a positive opportunity to build a better life.

Recent legislation has attempted to keep fathers involved with their children after divorce and to oblige them to maintain some financial responsibility for their children. In practice, the aims of the legislation have not fully been achieved, and the government is still seeking new ways of tackling the issue.

The picture that is emerging is one of children who wish to have their voices heard in decisions affecting their lives. They do not want the responsibility of choosing between parents, and they do not want the responsibility of the final say. But they do want their views to be taken into account. The old saying that 'children should be seen and not heard' has not yet entirely lost its force. The social construction of children as dependent and incompetent tends to militate against giving them full participation rights in matters affecting them. The Children Act (1989) allows children's wishes and feelings to be taken into account, but the means for ensuring this are inefficient, and the process of divorce remains firmly in the control of adults.

STUDY GUIDES

Group activities

1 Conduct some research in your class or college to find out whether romantic love is still important as the basis for intimate relationships. Do your findings support Giddens' argument about the transformation of intimacy?

2 Refer to recent *British Social Attitudes Surveys* to find out whether people continue to accord significance to marriage. In the light of your findings, discuss (a) why cohabitation seems to be on the increase and (b) why the divorce rate is so high.

3 In your group, consider the material in the previous chapter. Discuss whether Giddens' theory about the transformation of intimacy applies to both genders, to people in all social classes and ethnic groups.

Practice questions

Item A

Confluent love is active, contingent love, and therefore jars with the 'for–ever', 'one–and–only' qualities of the romantic love complex. The 'separating and divorcing society' of today here appears as an effect of the emergence of confluent love rather than its cause. The more confluent love becomes consolidated as a real possibility, the more the finding of a 'special person' recedes and the more it is the 'special relationship' that counts. In contrast to confluent love, romantic love has always been imbalanced in gender terms…For women, dreams of romantic love have all too often led to grim domestic subjugation. Confluent love presumes equality in emotional give and take.

Anthony Giddens, 1992, *The Transformation of Intimacy*, Polity, pp61–62.

Item B

According to a survey of 10-to-17-year-olds published today, most children believe that marriage should be for ever and that it is better to live with two parents than one. The *Reader's Digest* MORI poll comes as politicians and sociologists are struggling to come to terms with the changing nature of traditional family values. With right–wing policy makers casting single–parent families, rising divorce rates and the declining popularity of marriage as the root of many evils in modern British society, much has been claimed about the damaging effects on children. One survey suggests children accept that marriage does not always work. Nearly two thirds think couples should separate if they are unhappy. While nearly three-quarters said two parents were better than one, 45 per cent did not think it was wrong to have a child outside marriage … It seems children have not given up on marriage, with 82 per cent saying they were very likely or fairly likely to get married.

Flora Hunter, 1996 'Marriage still children's goal', in C. Donnellan (ed.) *Marriage and Divorce: Issues for the Nineties*, Independence Educational Publishers, p3.

Item C

Divorce is considered to be a risky business. Government, law and the professionals are expected to act to eliminate those risks. In the simplified version of child welfare knowledge, it is those children who are exposed to conflict or who are cut loose from fathers who are deemed to be most at risk psychologically, emotionally and economically. These are the risks, then, that have to be controlled. In constructing resident parents, and more particularly mothers, as having the power and the responsibility for decisions surrounding contact, the law, and the professionals, have succeeded in characterising them as posing the main risk to children. This has meant that mothers must be persuaded to make the 'right' decisions and, if necessary, their power has to be wrested from them by the courts … Contact with non–resident fathers and the reduction of conflict have come to be constructed as the solutions to what are regarded as some of the most serious problems of divorce.

Felicity Kaganas, 1999, 'Contact, conflict and risk', in S. Day Sclater and C. Piper (eds.) *Undercurrents of Divorce*, Ashgate, p115.

1 With reference to Item A and elsewhere, how does Giddens account for the 'separating and divorcing society'?

2 How might you reconcile the evidence indicated in Item B with Giddens' idea that love is losing its 'for–ever' quality?

3 With reference to Items A and C, assess the extent to which Giddens' thesis about the increasing popularity of confluent love is compatible with the lifestyles of women who have responsibility for children.

4 With reference to Item C and elsewhere, critically evaluate the claim that divorce is damaging to children.

5 With reference to Item C and elsewhere, give three reasons why divorce is a gender issue.

Coursework suggestions

1 How might you account for the increasing frequency of births outside marriage?

2 Why has divorce been seen as *the* social problem of our age?

3 How does divorce affect children? Can it ever be a positive experience?

7

PARENTS AND CHILDREN

Introduction

LIKE THE CONCEPT of 'family', the terms 'parents' and 'children' are not easy to define. Like 'family', they are familiar words, expressing identities with which we all have some acquaintance. We do not, in the ordinary course of things, stop to ponder the meanings of things so familiar. All that changes when we begin to study sociology. Sociology invites us to step back and to question those aspects of the social world that we normally take for granted. Considering the terms 'parents' and 'children' from a sociological perspective reveals the uncertain and fluid nature of these concepts, and the ways in which their meanings are apt to change over time, and to vary according to cultural context. In this chapter, we explore parenthood and childhood from a sociological perspective; we look at ideologies of the family in which particular images of parents and children are constructed, and consider a range of research studies that investigate the nature of parenthood and childhood in contemporary Britain.

PARENTS

As we saw in chapter 3, traditional Functionalist sociology of the family placed great emphasis on the work that parents do in socialising their children, and its contribution to the maintenance and reproduction of society. For the Functionalists, parental roles were strictly segregated along gender lines. This gendered division of labour in the family was assumed to reflect biological differences between women and men; each had a different contribution to make to family life, but the basis of their respective contributions was seen to lie in their

Table 8: *Key theorists, concepts and issues*		
KEY THEORISTS	KEY CONCEPTS	KEY ISSUES
Wilmott and Young	Parents	Are parenting behaviours natural? In what sense can they be said to be socially constructed?
K. Backett	Children	
C. Smart	Socialisation	What can anthropological evidence tell us about the nature of parenting?
James and Prout	Parental roles	
P. Aries	Family Law	
	Parental responsibility	Is parenting gender–neutral? Why has social science tended to neglect the study of fathers?
	Reproductive technologies	What are 'new' men?
	The social construction of childhood	What contribution does Family Law make to popular understandings of what parents are?
	Children's Rights	
		What significance do the new reproductive technologies have for our understanding of who parents are?
		What do sociologists mean when they say that childhood is socially constructed?
		Should children have the same rights as adults?
		What do sociologists mean when they talk about children's agency?

relationship to reproduction. In contrast to many other mammals, the human infant is born completely helpless and enjoys a prolonged period of dependency; without careful care and nurturing through the early years of life, it simply would not survive and our species would cease to exist. It has often been assumed that the patterns of women's mothering and men's fathering that predominate in industrialised Western cultures derive from these biological imperatives, but anthropological evidence suggests that, rather, parenting is *socially constructed* in different ways in different cultures.

ANTHROPOLOGICAL EVIDENCE

All human societies have institutionalised patterns of caring for the young, and research by anthropologists working in different cultures has revealed the great variety of ways in which the tasks of parenting are seen and carried out. Anthropological research indicates that the gender–based parenting practices that predominate in our society are by no means universal. For example, in hunter–gatherer societies such as the *Zhun/twasi* of Botswana, the !Kung women contribute more of the food consumed by the group than the men do. Both sexes are involved in child rearing and, unlike in the industrialised West, where children tend to be raised in relative isolation, child-rearing is a co–operative, community enterprise, and older children are also involved in caring for younger ones. In addition, !Kung women have closer and more prolonged physical contact with children who are nursed on demand and rarely left to cry. This kind of evidence casts doubt upon the assumption that biology exerts any determining influence on what men and women do as parents, and points instead towards understanding mothering and fathering as *socially organised* activities.

GENDER

Since the demise of Functionalism (see chapter 3), sociologists have been reluctant to accept the idea that any aspect of parenting is instinctual or biologically driven, and have preferred instead to talk about cultural influences on behaviours and the ways in which particular activities are socially organised, and parental identities socially constructed. From the 1960s onwards, sociologists of a feminist persuasion offered particularly trenchant criticisms of theories that seemed to 'naturalise' the social relations of parenting, arguing that such views represented ideological obstacles against women's full participation in public life and offending their basic rights as citizens. Feminists challenged the prevalent idea that 'biology is destiny' and showed, in empirical studies, that 'maternal instinct' was difficult to find; for most women bearing their first child, mothering behaviour seemed rather to be something that was slowly, and often painfully, learned. Feminist sociologists also exposed ideas about the 'perfect mother' as myths — idealised fantasies that concealed unrealistic expectations of what mothers could do, and provided a basis for 'mother-blaming' whenever things went wrong. These kind of feminist challenges to prevailing orthodoxies have helped to focus attention on the ways in which biological differences themselves are necessarily socially organised in any cultural setting. We may all be biological beings, but our biology is never expressed simply and directly; rather, the meanings that attach to biology are derived from culture. Those meanings are apt to change as society evolves, and can even be a matter for individual negotiation across a single lifetime.

Study point

Make a list of the things you would expect women as mothers to do. Make another list for fathers, and compare the two. What can you conclude about the gendered nature of parenting?

CONTEMPORARY VIEWS

Contemporary sociologists therefore recognise that there are both biological and social aspects to parenting, and that it is difficult, perhaps impossible, to separate the two. Empirical studies show that men and women do respond differently to babies and children. For example, mothers in a range of different cultures have been shown to exaggerate their facial expressions and alter their speech with babies, without realising that they do it. This tendency is also evident in young girls, but much less pronounced in men and boys. This does not indicate, however, that females are doing this because they are biologically uniquely equipped to do so; such behaviours can be part of the unconscious learning that goes on every day of our lives. This is also supported by empirical work which has demonstrated that people respond differently to boy and girl babies, being more likely to cuddle and verbalise softly towards girl babies, and more likely to be physical and playful towards a boy. Thus it seems that boy and girl babies are exposed from very early on to differential treatment on the basis of their assumed gender.

The Ideology of Parenting

Parenting today remains a largely gendered activity; in the main, it is mothers who do the bulk of the caring and nurturing activities in the home. This is so even where both parents go out to work. The ideology of parenting is moving rapidly towards gender neutrality, but the practice of parenting is somewhat different. Sociological studies show that when women work outside the home, the expectations upon them at home as regards housework and childcare do not decrease. These activities continue to consume between 40 and 70 hours per week, with women doing the bulk of the work. The male partners of working women do contribute more to housework and child care than they did a generation ago, but their contribution tends to be in terms of 'helping' whilst taking overall responsibility is still women's work. The average woman works outside the home for wages and then comes home to tackle the unpaid work — what Hochschild calls the 'second shift'. A cursory look at contemporary 'parenting' magazines and literature reveals the continuing centrality of women to children's lives; the magazines, and the advertisements they contain, are clearly directed at the female consumer, and images of men are rare.

Study point

- Can children be cared for by women and men with equal ease and competence?

FATHERS

Until very recently, sociological work on fathers has been conspicuous by its absence. It was not until the 1980s that social scientists began to turn their attention to fathers; until then, work on parents was really work on mothers. This has been partly a result of the dominance of a particular ideology of motherhood that saw only mothers as centrally important to children's development. In part, it is also a legacy of a long tradition in psychology, from Freud onwards, that saw fathers as peripheral in child development. The primary attachment bond was seen to be that between the mother and the child; at most, the father was mentioned in his role as helpmate and support for the mother. All that is now changing. It is probably accurate to say that it was concern over the effects of divorce on children that provided the impetus for a new social scientific interest in fathers. A prime concern has been father–absence, to which has been attributed a range of social ills from educational under–achievement to juvenile crime.

Ideologies of fatherhood are beginning to change, but it is doubtful how far these new ideas about 'new' nurturing and home–oriented men reflect the realities of fatherhood today. Important sociological work done by Wilmott and Young in the London's East End in the 50s and 60s found that some fathers were taking on a greater share of what had previously been women's tasks. Ideas about the companionate marriage and the symmetrical family (see chapter 3) assumed an increasing egalitarianism in the home; some sociologists argued that gender divisions in the home were being eroded, while more decisions were being made jointly, resources were being shared more equally, and that household tasks were becoming increasingly likely to be shared. However, others have pointed out that such changes can only be found in a minority of families and that such ideas present, not a picture of reality, but an idealised version of middle–class life that is not even evident in the majority of middle–class households. The 'new' man has been said to be more a figment of the media's imagination than a reality, even as we enter the twenty-first century. The consensus among sociologists is that social change in patterns of fathering is actually occurring much slower than we might like it to be.

Sociologists argue that ideologies of fatherhood are changing. Discuss this issue in your group, and speculate what the father role will be like in 50 years time.

Sociologist Kathryn Backett makes an important point: she argues that a father's relationship to his children is mediated by the mother; it is something that is negotiated with the mother, rather than constituting an independent relationship with the children. In other words, fatherhood does not have an autonomous existence in the way that motherhood has. In practice, this means that active, hands–on parenting is required of mothers, but it is optional for fathers, and whether it happens or not depends, in large part, on the active co–operation of the mother. This important finding has obvious implications when trying to understand why it is that, on divorce, so many men fade out of their children's lives. Other sociologists have argued that for men, being a father is closely linked with the marital status of husband; on divorce, fatherhood is therefore difficult to sustain, however attached the man may be to the children. Mothers never cease being mothers whereas, for men, being a father is contingent upon other relationships and strongly influenced by circumstantial factors.

FAMILY LAW

Despite changing ideologies, therefore, parenting remains an activity that is deeply infused with the social relations of gender. In this context, the fact that parenting is actively constructed in a gender neutral way by family law is somewhat anomalous. The Children Act 1989 created a new concept, that of 'parental responsibility', which gave married parents equal rights to a say in major decisions affecting the lives of their children, and which is retained by both mothers and fathers, despite divorce. One of the aims of the legislation was to encourage greater continuing responsibility for children on the part of fathers. The legislation is founded on an assumption of gender neutral parenting; that children can equally easily and competently be cared for by mothers and fathers, and that neither should be favoured over the other when making decisions about with whom the child should live or whom the child should visit.

The legislation aimed to secure the continuance of family relationships and to facilitate co–operative co–parenting after divorce when the parents were living in separate households. However, there is little evidence that these aims are being met. On the contrary, recent research shows that disputes over children are increasing in frequency, and that cases are taking longer to be resolved. One explanation for this unfortunate state of affairs is that our legislators have presumed too much, and have failed to take account of social and scientific evidence that motherhood and fatherhood are complex activities that remain highly gendered. If Backett is right in saying that fatherhood during the subsistence of a marriage is highly dependent upon the facilitating activities of mothers, then it should come as no surprise that, on divorce, when parents are likely to feel hurt and angry with each other, that co–operation breaks down.

Study point
What happens to parenting when mothers and fathers live in separate households?

Divorced fathers are faced with the daunting prospect of having to develop a new kind of independent relationship with the children, without the mother's facilitating presence. It is not surprising that many men find it difficult to carve out a new terrain for themselves as fathers. The assumptions in the Children Act that parenting can simply carry on as before are undermined by the sociological evidence. As sociologist Carol Smart argues, many of the problems that divorcing parents face have their origins in the wider society, and in the ideologies and social relations of gender; family law is ill–equipped to address such issues. In this context, she says, family law provisions for equal, joint parenting after divorce sit very uneasily with economic and employment policies that make it practically impossible for the majority to practice joint parenting even during marriage.

Activity
Refer to the Children Act 1989 and find a definition for 'parental responsibility'. Decide whether you think the definition adequately captures what you think of as parental responsibility.

NEW REPRODUCTIVE TECHNOLOGIES

Since the birth of the first 'test-tube baby' in 1978, there has been a rapid proliferation of reproductive technologies that make it possible for people to become parents who otherwise could not have done so. For many, these technologies have provided a welcome solution to problems of infertility. But, techniques for egg and sperm donation, in–vitro fertilisation (IVF) and surrogacy have brought other problems in their wake.

These developments are introducing new issues into sociological debates about parenthood, and new levels of confusion into legal debates about who should count as a 'parent' in law. The recent availability of DNA testing, by which paternity can be definitively established by matching gene sequences from fathers against those of children, has been widely used in connection with the Child Support Act as a way of determining the identity of the man who has to make financial provision for a child. The new emphasis on genetic connections is undoubtedly influencing contemporary constructions of parents in biological terms. In most cases, there is little doubt about who is the mother of a particular child — it is she who gives birth to the child — but certainty about paternity is not so straightforward. Traditionally, fathers have been deemed to be those who were married to the mother at the time the child was conceived, and family law has operated in support of this presumption. However, as we have seen, an increasing number of children are being born outside of marriage, and it is in this context that questions about who the father is arise. Sociologists have noted the ascendancy of models of family life that venerate biologically–related kin, and have argued that, in the face of a declining marriage rate, parenthood has begun to supersede marriage as the basis for family status. Society now seems to accept that marriage may no longer be 'for life'; in its place, biological parenthood now occupies a distinctive status. A biological connection between a parent and a child can now form the basis of a legal claim to have a relationship with that child (under the Children Act, 1989) as well as a responsibility financially to support that child (under the Child Support Act, 1991). Biology and, increasingly, genetics now provide the main basis upon which claims to parental status rest.

Challenges to the Concept of Parent

However, these developments exist in considerable tension with others that have broadened the concept of 'parent' as a social status. Step–parents, foster parents, adoptive parents, the parents of children born of egg and sperm donation, and parents of children born of surrogacy arrangements do not necessarily have any biological connection with the child, yet they are recognised in law as parents. These parents can be seen as 'social' parents, who make a vital contribution to their children's development, although they need not have any biological connection to them. These parents have rights and responsibilities in law that, in many instances, are comparable to those of parents who are biologically related.

Developments in biomedical technologies, particularly cloning, seem set to compound the issue of who parents are even further. Although cloning for reproductive purposes is not currently legal in Britain, we do possess the technologies to clone people, in the same way that Dolly the sheep was cloned. At present, cloning is only legal for research purposes, and cloned human embryos must be destroyed before they are two weeks old. This raises a number of ethical problems that are beyond the scope of this book. What is important for us is that the development of biomedical technologies currently provides us with the means for creating children who have more than two biological parents; cloning (or cell nucleus replacement techniques) has the capacity to produce offspring with multiple genetic parents, not just two oppositely sexed ones.

DOLLY – THE WORLD'S FIRST CLONE OF AN ADULT ANIMAL. BIOMEDICAL TECHNOLOGIES MAY, IN THE FUTURE, HOLD FAR-REACHING IMPLICATIONS FOR 'THE FAMILY' AND ITS EVER-CHANGING FORMS.

Study point

Would it be possible to clone a human being in the same way that Dolly the sheep was cloned?

CHILDREN

In chapter 6 we introduced the idea that 'childhood' is socially constructed. This is an idea that is currently popular in sociology and, as James and Prout point out, it refers to the way in which immaturity may be a biological fact, but the meanings attributed to such immaturity are not biologically determined, but are derived from culture. The study of childhood is now a sociological topic in its own right, and research centres have been set up across the country to investigate the nature of childhood and to begin to listen to what children themselves say about their lives.

The concept of childhood is something that has changed historically and that varies from culture to culture. According to social historian Phillipe Aries, the model of childhood that is dominant today only emerged in Europe in roughly the 18th century; before that, it seems that there was little concept of children as being fundamentally different from adults. As Pollock argues, however, it is important not to lose sight of the many continuities in the history of childhood. This historical work shows that how we conceptualise children is very much rooted in the social and economic circumstances of particular epochs. This is another instance of sociology obliging us to question our taken–for–granted assumptions about how the world is. We all think that we know what a child is when we see one, but that very familiarity evidences the dominant ideologies of our culture, and places obstacles in the way of questioning why and how we have come to regard children in the way that we ordinarily do.

Activity
What does historical research tell us about the nature of childhood?

When we looked at divorce, in chapter 6, we noted that there was a particular model of childhood that seemed to inform the debates. In both family law provisions and research on divorce, we saw an image of children emerging that portrayed them as vulnerable 'victims', without any say in the decisions that affected them. We noted the ways in which such an image linked into broader cultural conceptions of childhood. Sociologists have argued that such images do children a disservice, and serve to render children, as a social group, marginal and powerless in relation to adults. Some sociologists have begun to study the way that children themselves see their worlds, and to document how things look from children's own perspectives. Central to this new enterprise in sociology has been a conception of children, not as the passive recipients of what adults do, but as active human agents in their own right. For example, sociologist and anthropologist Virginia Morrow has studied what children think about families. Her main finding was that children conceptualise families, not in terms of structure or function (as sociologists are prone to do), but in terms of relationships; children include, in their concepts of family, people who are important to them and with whom they have meaningful relationships. Thus many children include 'pets' when asked who is in their family. These are important findings, and they signify a challenge to traditional sociological work that has failed to inquire about how children themselves see things. Similarly, as we have seen in relation to divorce, a few sociologists are beginning to address the issue of what children themselves say and feel.

SOCIAL CONSTRUCTION OF CHILDHOOD

Sociologists Allison James and Alan Prout have been at the forefront of those who advocate seeing childhood as socially constructed. They point out that traditional sociology has tended to regard children as passive and as lacking any agency of their own. For example, the Functionalist discussions about familial 'roles' and about 'socialisation' tend to position children as the passive recipients of society's needs and adults' demands. What is left out is children's own agency, and their capacities for relationships, and needs and desires of their own. Sociologists have also pointed out that children tend to have been studied outside of their ordinary family lives when, in fact, childhood is intimately connected to families; what goes on in families is of profound significance to children and to their development and, conversely, children themselves actually play a significant part in family life. These sociologists, of a more critical persuasion, also point out that 'parenting' is seen as something that is *done to* children whereas, from a child's perspective, it is a negotiated enterprise, in which children play their part.

These sociologists have made an essential contribution in undermining traditional notions about the meanings of childhood and in introducing ideas about children as human citizens. Significantly, too, they have reminded us that the concept of childhood is socially constructed rather than a natural state. What each society thinks about children is more a reflection of the values of that society than it is a reflection of the intrinsic nature of childhood.

Activity
In what ways do children differ from adults? Make a list, and compare with other students.

CHANGING ROLE OF CHILDREN

Certainly, the role of children in families and society has changed historically; and their ability to contribute to household economies has diminished in accordance with restrictions on the legal age at which children can engage in remunerative work. In parallel, families have become more child–centred and the period of dependence for children and adolescents upon their parents has become more prolonged, along with changes in the education system and the availability of paid work for young people. Sociologists would argue that the opportunities for young people to lead independent and economically productive lives have diminished as the emphasis on education has grown, accompanied by changing ideologies that position children as dependent and vulnerable.

The 'welfare of children' has become a priority in social policy, and currently our society provides a vast array of initiatives and provisions designed to ensure that children are protected from the worst abuses of both public (the world of work) and private (the family) life. Importantly, however, in all these provisions is an image of children as vulnerable and of requiring protection. Sociologists look to these sorts of provisions and conclude that they provide evidence that contemporary notions of childhood are socially produced and that they fit with broader ideologies of parenting and family life.

THE PROBLEM OF CHILD ABUSE

The current emphasis on children and on the need for families and society to prioritise their welfare, however, sits somewhat uneasily with the realisation that some children are abused in families and in the care system. In the 1970s, the physical abuse of children in their families reared its ugly head as a major social problem. In the 1980s, there was widespread concern about sexual abuse, and in the 1990s the category of abuse has been expanded to include emotional abuse. The social visibility of such personal problems (which we discuss in more detail in chapter 9) has intensified sociological debates about the nature of family life. Families, once idealistically portrayed as safe havens, appear in the light of the abuse statistics as potentially very dangerous places for children. The problems of child abuse are difficult to investigate by social scientists because they are so intensely personal; these issues inevitably arouse feelings on the part of researchers, who understandably find it difficult to conduct their studies in a wholly objective and dispassionate way.

Despite this, sociologists have been at the forefront of those who have documented the problems of child abuse in families. They have also critically analysed the solutions society has provided for these problems. The primary form of social response to the problem of child abuse has been the child protection system, implemented by social workers, with the support of the courts. Children who are suspected of being abused can become the subject of public law proceedings that identify them as 'at risk', or can remove them from their families and place them into care, into foster homes or accommodation provided by the local authority. Sadly, there have been a number of recent, disturbing reports of children who have been further abused whilst in the care of the local authority. Thankfully, this only occurs in a small minority of cases, but perhaps these cases serve to highlight a broader problem, namely the social construction of children as a vulnerable and incompetent group.

Some sociologists argue that the dominant image of children, as innocent, vulnerable and in need of adult protection, is the very thing that predisposes children to abuse by adults. On this view, our child protection system is more a part of the problem of child abuse than it is a solution to it. If, for example, we readily heard children's voices, and listened to what they had to say, we would render them less vulnerable to abuse by adults. If we invested children with autonomy and the ability to say 'no', and to be taken notice of, adults would find it so much more difficult to exploit them sexually or abuse them physically. If children had participation and citizenship rights on a par with those of adults, they would have a clearer voice in which to express themselves and their needs.

CHILDREN'S RIGHTS

In 1989, the United Nations adopted the Convention on the Rights of the Child. By 1996, this had been ratified by 186 of the 190 member states. The Convention establishes the rights of children to care and protection, and to be active participants in the society in which they live. Therefore, in countries that have ratified the convention, children must be protected from harm and must be treated with the respect accorded to autonomous citizens. In practice, however, the Convention seems to have made little impact. In Britain, for example, it has not been formally adopted by the statutory agencies who are responsible for children's welfare. Parents, and the State, still have the power to determine what is in a child's best interests; they are likely to be influenced by the dominant view of children in our society which we discussed earlier. In other words, as long as we maintain a vision of children as dependent and incompetent, we are unlikely to accord to them the kinds of rights that the UN Convention provides for. In Britain, the dominant welfare ideology militates against the achievement of true participation rights and citizenship for children.

Activity

Refer to the United Nations Convention on the Rights of the Child. Describe the range of rights that it gives to children. List the factors that you think might militate against the exercise of those rights in practice.

SUMMARY

'Parents' and 'children' are interdependent terms, that are not easy to define. They are concepts whose meaning is apt to change according to history and social context. Sociologists commonly refer to parenthood and childhood as being socially constructed. In any society, there are dominant ideas about what parents are and what they should do in order to be good parents. There are similar ideas about what children are. In industrialised societies, the relationship between adults and children is a hierarchical one, with adults having the power and greater access to resources. By contrast, children are seen as innocent and vulnerable, as lacking the capacity to make important decisions, and as requiring the protection of adults and the State.

Functionalist sociologists pointed to the importance of the socialising functions of the family, executed through the activities of parents. For them, parental roles were strictly segregated along gender lines, and this was seen to reflect the natural order of things. Anthropological evidence, however, indicated that parenting behaviours were socially organised in different ways in different cultures, and therefore could not just reflect biological imperatives. Sociological evidence shows that what women and men do as mothers and fathers is different; mothers and fathers are not just interchangeable and each make a different contribution to their children's lives and development.

Sociological studies of motherhood were popular in the 1970s, and in the 1980s the interest extended to fathers too. Traditionally, fathers have been regarded as less central than mothers to children's development, but this idea is now changing, as are ideologies of masculinity. Recently, the 'new' man who adopts more of a nurturing and caring role in the family, has been the subject of much media speculation and sociological debate. Nevertheless, evidence suggests that these changes are slow to take hold, and parenting continues to be a highly gendered activity.

Despite this, Family Law has sought, through its concept of 'parental responsibility', to regard parenting as gender neutral and to allocate the same rights and responsibilities to mothers and fathers. Some feminist sociologists have been very critical of this development, arguing that it ignores the fact that women continue to do the bulk of parenting work.

In recent years, the proliferation of new reproductive technologies has enabled some infertile people to become parents, but these technologies also introduce new problems. For example, using IVF and egg donation it is possible for a woman to give birth to a child that is not genetically related to her. In surrogacy arrangements a child is passed, at or shortly after birth, to the 'commissioning parents' to bring up as their own. In instances like this, defining who the 'parents' are cannot be done with simple reference to genetic relationships, but must instead be based on social relationships. Cloning and cell nuclear transfer techniques (currently outlawed in Britain for reproductive purposes) permit the possibility of creating a child with more than two genetic parents.

Sociologists argue that childhood is socially constructed. By this they mean that children's immaturity is a biological fact, but the meanings and values that are attached to that immaturity are facts of culture. In our society, a particular view of children as innocent, vulnerable and incompetent prevails. The United Nations Convention of the Rights of the Child gives children some rights, but they still lack the full participation rights that adult citizens have. This situation is unlikely to change unless ideologies of childhood change too.

STUDY GUIDES

Group activities

1 In your group, discuss what Backett means when she says that a father's relationship to his children is mediated by the mother. If Backett is right, what are the implications for divorce?
2 Conduct a class debate: This house believes that the production of human beings by cloning will be commonplace in the next century.
3 Conduct some research in your class to find out what other students think children's rights are. Work together to devise a questionnaire that could be used to find out what children themselves think their rights are.

Practice questions

Item A

In this case, whilst there is no doubt the mother is a good mother in one sense of the word in that she looks after the children well, giving them love and, as far as she can, security, one must remember that to be a good mother involves not only looking after the children, but making and keeping a home for them with their father ... In so far as she herself by her own conduct broke up that home, she is not a good mother.
Lord Denning MR in the case of Re L [1962] 1WLR, pp.889–890.

Item B

Of considerable interest in Backett's research was her discovery that fathers did not have to do equal amounts of caring in order to be regarded as good fathers ... This child rearing was often described as being equally shared, when in fact it was nothing of the sort. In a way this is perhaps not surprising — at least in intact households. The mother may well regard the father's full time job as an important contribution to the family's well–being and thus would hardly expect him to carry an equal responsibility for routine child–rearing. In our sample we found that almost all the parents voiced a firm belief that there was really no difference between a 'good' mother and a 'good' father. Both were seen as good if they provided a high quality relationship for the child. This was expressed in terms of providing love, 'being there' for the children and giving them security. At the level of rhetoric our parents seemed to suggest that mothers and fathers were interchangeable in principle — at least when they were asked a direct question about mothering and fathering. But when it came to specifics this account was modified somewhat, usually with fathers asserting that there is no difference between a mother and a father, but with mothers diverging from this account and offering what they would see as a more 'factual' account of how mother and father operate.
Carol Smart and Bren Neale, 1999, *Family Fragments?*, Polity Press, p.48.

Item C

Some writing is explicitly hostile to the children's rights project on the basis that it undermines the integrity of the family (Burrows, 1998). Just as the language of the 'best interests of the child' was used to legitimate a range of state sanctioned interventions into family life, likewise today the language of children's rights is seen as a kind of late twentieth century 'Trojan horse'. Arguments around the parental right to chastise their child and to bring up their children as they see fit, free from the risk of state interference save in clearly defined circumstances, connect with wider arguments on state power, images of 'big brother' (or the 'nanny state') and the right of families and the communities within which they live their lives to live these lives differently.

Jeremy Roche, 1999, 'Children and Divorce: A private affair?', in S. Day Sclater and C. Piper (eds.) *Undercurrents of Divorce*, Ashgate, p60.

1 With reference to Item A and elsewhere, assess whether a judge today would be likely to make similar assumptions about what it means to be a 'good mother'.

2 With reference to Items A and B, list three arguments for and three arguments against the claim that mothers and fathers are interchangeable.

3 With reference to Item B and elsewhere, give three reasons why the ideal of co–parenting after divorce is difficult to achieve in practice.

4 With reference to Item C and elsewhere, give three reasons why there has been resistance to children's rights.

5 With reference to Items A, B and C and elsewhere, describe the dominant image of children in contemporary Britain, and explain how it is linked to ideologies of parenting and the family.

Coursework suggestions

1 Write an essay entitled: Which is more important, the biological tie or the social relationship between children and their parents?

2 Discuss the old saying: 'Children should be seen and not heard'. Consider what changes might help children's own voices to be heard more effectively.

3 Evaluate the evidence for and against the proposition that parenting is a gender neutral activity.

8

FAMILY PROBLEMS

Introduction

ALTHOUGH THE FAMILY has traditionally been seen as a private place, a safe haven from the strains of the outside world, sociologists have increasingly drawn attention to the family as a location for violence and abuse, particularly against women and children. Sociologists have highlighted the darker side of family life that exists in contradiction to prevailing ideologies of 'home sweet home'. Whereas those in the Functionalist school saw the family as a *functional unit*, other sociologists have stressed that families can often be *dysfunctional*, failing to meet the needs of individual family members and, in some cases, actually causing damage. Functionalists tended to characterise the family as a coherent, unified interest group and family relationships as harmonious. For them, family problems were essentially *private troubles* and so did not threaten their basic premises about the family as a functional unit for society.

Critics of the Functionalist position have responded by pointing out that these assumptions about coherence, unity and harmony reflect, not the realities of family life, but an *ideal* of how society would like families to be. They argue that problems in families, such as domestic violence and child abuse, are not just private troubles but are related to the hierarchical power structures in families and, as such, are actually *social problems*. These sociologists point out that real families consist of different, and sometimes competing, interest groups.

For example, the family is segregated along age lines; adults exercise power and authority over children, and the interests of adults in the family do not always coincide with those of children (this observation becomes particularly significant in connection with divorce). As we have seen, the family is also segregated along gender lines; in many families men and women have differential access to

Table 9: *Key concepts and issues*	
KEY CONCEPTS	KEY ISSUES
Domestic violence Child abuse Dysfunctional families Power relationships Patriarchy	How should domestic violence be defined? Should the definition encompass emotional as well as physical and sexual abuse? What kinds of legal protections are available for women who are abused by their partners? How prevalent is domestic violence? How should domestic violence be explained? What could be done to prevent it? Why do some women stay in violent relationships? How have definitions of child abuse changed over time? How should child abuse be explained? What could be done to prevent it?

resources and what may be in the interests of men in the household, may not be in the interests of the women. Sociologists, particularly those of a feminist persuasion, have argued that these issues of power relationships in families underlie a range of family problems. These problems are the subject of this chapter. We look in some detail at domestic violence and child abuse, and at the links between them, and we consider the implications for family sociology of understanding family problems as fundamentally connected to social structures and gendered ideologies and practices.

DOMESTIC VIOLENCE

Traditionally, the law saw men as the undisputed heads of households, and permitted them to 'correct' and 'chastise' women and children in the family. Women and men were not equal in the eyes of the law, and husbands could legitimately exercise control over their wives, for example, by confining them to the home. These were the days when divorce was extremely rare and prohibitively expensive for the majority of people. Thus, many women were trapped in unhappy, even abusive, marriages with little hope of getting away. Feminist sociologists refer to this system of male domination, sanctified by law, as *patriarchy*, and for a long time women's groups have campaigned for equality and for a right to legal protection from abuse and violence in the home. Beginning in Victorian times, the law has gradually changed to accord greater rights to women (and, more recently, to children) and to offer them protection from the worst abuses of male power. It was not until the 1970s, however, that domestic violence and child abuse became publicly visible as problems demanding some attention. Since then, campaigners for women's and children's rights have lobbied successive governments, seeking some recognition of the problem and calling for more effective measures to tackle it.

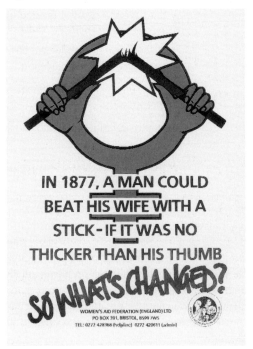

IN 1877, A MAN COULD
BEAT HIS WIFE WITH A
STICK - IF IT WAS NO
THICKER THAN HIS THUMB
SO WHAT'S CHANGED?

WOMEN'S AID FEDERATION (ENGLAND) LTD
PO BOX 391, BRISTOL, BS99 7WS
TEL: 0272 428368 (helpline) 0272 420611 (admin)

A WOMEN'S AID FEDERATION POSTER – HIGHLIGHTING THE STILL PRESENT PROBLEM OF DOMESTIC VIOLENCE.

A major turning point occurred in 1971 when Erin Pizzey set up the first refuge for 'battered women' in Chiswick, London. Since then, Women's Aid has expanded and is now a national enterprise with safe refuges all over the country for women and their children trying to escape from abuse by male partners. In 1976, the civil law was reformed to permit abused women to apply to the court for protection from molestation (*injunctions*) or to remove the abuser from the home (*ouster orders*). Most recently, the law was reformed again in 1996, to expand the category of people who could benefit from such protection and to make available a greater range of remedies. Legal Aid is available to people of limited means to assist them in bringing legal proceedings to protect themselves and/or their children. In addition, people who are abused in the home may also benefit from the operation of the criminal law. Violence in a domestic context amounts to criminal assault, and perpetrators can be arrested, prosecuted and imprisoned.

The efficacy of both civil and criminal procedures in tackling the problem of domestic violence, however, is a subject of some dispute among sociologists. Some would argue that the available court orders are hardly worth the paper they are written on, that they can have the effect of making the violent partner even more angry, that they are routinely broken, and that the courts are reluctant to enforce them, except in very extreme cases. Others would argue that court orders can help, and that they have great symbolic value in making the point to the perpetrator that society sees domestic violence as unacceptable, and in indicating to the victim that they are entitled to, and worthy of, the court's protection.

Study point

In your group, discuss whether the legal protections currently available in cases of domestic violence are adequate. Consider what else might be done to protect women who are abused.

The criminal law in relation to violence in the home has had something of a chequered history. It has long been a criminal offence to assault, hurt or wound another person, including someone you live with or are married to. Yet, the police have tended not to regard domestic violence as on a par with other forms of violence; the latter they have traditionally regarded as being much more serious than the former. A few years ago, it was common for police, called out to homes where there had been violent incidents, to regard them as 'only domestics', with prosecutions rarely following. This situation is now changing, and many police forces now have specialised personnel for dealing with these types of cases, and are developing a deeper understanding of the nature of the problem. Sociologists have been in the forefront of those who have contributed to this understanding. Sociological research, for example, has helped to clarify the causes of violence and to suggest remedies. It has also assisted in broadening our understanding of the effects of violence, and the reasons why victims have often been reluctant to pursue civil remedies or criminal prosecutions.

DEFINING DOMESTIC VIOLENCE

The first problem that faces a sociologist interested in domestic violence is that of how to define their topic of study. Some behaviours, such as punching and kicking, would easily be recognised as violent by the law, but other behaviours such as issuing threats, verbal abuse, psychological manipulation and some forms of sexual behaviour are more ambiguous. Overt physical and sexual assault will attract legal protection that is much less likely to be available in relation to the more ambiguous forms of abuse in the home. Overwhelmingly, domestic assaults are attacks by men on women; there is a strongly gendered element to the problem. Undoubtedly some women also hurt their male partners, but sociologists would argue that the meanings of male and female violence are different. Male violence is usually *instrumental*, in that it is linked to men's attempts to maintain control over women and to enforce their authority in the home. Women's violence is more likely to be *defensive*; it is not intended to induce fear or to maintain subordination, but to be used in self–defence, once a fight starts.

Study point

- How effective are injunctions in stopping domestic violence?
- Can men who hit their wives be arrested?

THE INCIDENCE OF DOMESTIC VIOLENCE

It is, of course, impossible to accurately assess the true numbers of violent episodes that occur in homes up and down the country, as it remains largely a 'hidden' problem, taking place behind closed doors, often with no witnesses present. However, based on surveys and crime statistics, sociologists have estimated that one out of four married women are likely to experience violence. Currently, it is women who most often initiate divorce proceedings, and most of those do so on the basis of allegations about the husband's 'unreasonable behaviour', a legal category that includes physical, psychological and sexual violence. Violence by men against their female partners accounts for about a third of all reported violence. Seventy per cent of reported domestic violence is violence by men against their female partners, whilst only one per cent is that by wives against their husbands. These figures are undoubtedly underestimates of the true extent of the problem, since much violence still goes unreported.

THE CAUSES OF VIOLENCE

Sociological work has made a considerable contribution to our understanding of the causes of violence in the home. Below, we will consider *four* models that have been put forward to account for the causes of violence.

Male aggression is natural. This model proposes that violence is best explained with reference to biology. Human beings, the argument goes, are biological creatures that share some characteristics with other mammals. Male animals are habitually more aggressive than females ones, and this propensity for aggression manifests itself in human society in the form of domestic violence. From a sociological viewpoint, however, this model does not stand up to scrutiny. Sociologists argue that humans may be animals, but the influences of society and culture on human behaviour means that it is not on a par with animal behaviour. If humans can be said to have such things as instincts, these must always be mediated by social practices and cultural values. Human beings are fully conscious and self–conscious, they are capable of rational thought, have memories and can make plans for the future. These characteristics lie at the base of human societies and are what distinguish us from animals. From a sociological point of view, therefore, the idea that men have natural instincts for aggression, as an explanation of domestic violence, is inadequate.

Violence reflects individual pathology. This model assumes that individual perpetrators must be disturbed in some way, and that their behaviour reflects some underlying pathology. It therefore assumes that there are significant differences between 'abnormal' men who abuse their partners and those 'normal' men who do not. Dobash and Dobash, for instance, have suggested that abusive men tend to have had insecure childhoods, and that it is their unmet dependency needs that express themselves in violence in adult life. Psychodynamic theories lend some support to this model. They suggests that male children are socialised to become independent and to deny their vulnerable feelings; in this way, men can come to fear dependency and may lash out aggressively if they are reminded of their own needs and vulnerabilities, as frequently happens in intimate relationships. Sociologists say, however, that it is important not to individualise the problem of domestic violence, and that it is necessary to take account of the influence of society and culture on patterns of violence. The problem of domestic violence should not be 'reduced' to one of individual pathology, and it is necessary to bear in mind that society is strongly implicated in the values that are accorded to masculinity. If male children are socialised to deny their vulnerable feelings, this is more a problem of our society's structures and values, than it is of individual pathologies.

Violence reflects disturbed interactional patterns between partners. This model suggests that violence is a product of pathological interactions between two people; one is as much to blame as the other for its occurrence. Thus, couples may be seen as simply 'bad for each other', as 'rubbing each other up the wrong way', as having poor communication skills, or as having incompatible personalities that constitute an unstable, volatile partnership, apt to explode at any time. Each partner, consciously or unconsciously, upsets and provokes the other, until a violent episode ensues. On this model, violence is a mutual phenomenon, in which both partners carry blame. Again, this model is supported by psychodynamic theories that see couples as having unconsciously selected each other, influenced by the need to work through unresolved developmental conflicts from childhood and infancy. Sociologists recognise that this model has some explanatory power in helping us to understand how conflict escalates and can end in violence, but it does not really explain the gendered dimension of the problem.

Domestic violence reflects gendered power differences. This is the model preferred by feminist sociologists. Yllo, for example, suggests that the beating of an individual wife by an individual husband is not an individual or even a family problem. Rather it is a problem of patriarchy, of male domination. On this view, *all* men, and not just a few disturbed ones, have the capacity for violence and *all* women are at risk. Violence is something that *normal* men can resort to, if their needs are not met or their expectations are thwarted. Empirical sociological studies offer some support for this model. For instance, research has shown that men's perception that women have failed to carry out their duties, to men's satisfaction, is regarded by many violent men as legitimate grounds for argument, accusations and attacks. Violent episodes are often fuelled by drink, but this is not always the case. Sexual jealousy can also be an important precipitating factor. This model reminds us that the gendered roles that society prescribes for women and men in families, lead to expectations which, if they aren't met, can provoke outbreaks of hostilities that can end in violence. Today, although many women go out to work, men still tend to have more material and ideological power than women. With this backdrop, violence can be a way of exerting control and maintaining power. It is therefore a *social problem* that has its roots in gendered ideologies and in continuing material inequalities.

Activity
List four models that have been proposed to account for the causes of domestic violence. Which do you think is the most plausible, and why?

WHY MIGHT WOMEN STAY IN VIOLENT RELATIONSHIPS?

This feminist model also suggests some reasons why women do not always leave violent relationships. Women who are materially dependant on a violent man may feel they have no alternative but to put up with it, and many are also fearful of the consequences for their children if they were to leave. In recent years, the idea that 'families need fathers' and that the presence of fathers, even violent ones, are essential to children's healthy development, has gained in prominence, and seems likely to provide further reasons why some women stay in violent relationships. In addition, abused women can come to suffer from what psychologists have called 'learned helplessness' as a result of the abuse they suffer, leading to lowered feelings of self–worth and a felt inability to do anything that can change the situation. Evidence suggests, however, that these women do not 'give up' easily, that they actively seek help, but cannot always get the legal, social and material support they need to end the relationship.

In some extreme cases, abused women have responded by killing their attackers. In some instances they have been found guilty of murder or manslaughter and have been imprisoned. In a few cases, however, they have been acquitted, and the courts have taken into account the effects of prolonged victimisation on their mental state. The courts are now prepared, in some cases, to recognise 'battered woman syndrome' as a special category of psychiatric illness, whereby the balance of the victim's mind is seen to have been disturbed as a result of the violence she has suffered. The syndrome has been invoked in criminal prosecutions to account for the victim's eventual retaliation.

For Black women, the problems of violence in the home can be compounded by racial prejudice. Black women may already lack trust in the police who may be regarded as racist. They may therefore be less likely to seek the assistance of the police if they are attacked. If the police are called, they may be operating with implicit ideas about Black people, and may fail to properly understand what has happened. Mama reports, for example, that Black women trying to flee from violent men experienced far less helpful responses from a local housing department than did White women. She also notes that the refuge system can unwittingly discriminate against Black women in terms of the assistance they provide. In recent years, some new refuges have been set up by Black women specifically for Black women, to deal with their particular needs and to protect them against the added violence and pain of racial discrimination.

CHILD ABUSE

In the early 1970s Kempe and Kempe brought the problem of the *physical abuse* of children out into the open and into widespread public awareness and debate.

This was followed, in the 1980s, by a new visibility for *sexual abuse*. The Cleveland Crisis, in 1987, in which large numbers of children were removed from their parents on suspicion of having been sexually abused, was widely debated in the media and drew the attention of the public to a social problem on a scale hitherto unheard of. The 1990s has seen a further widening of the category of abuse, to include *emotional abuse*, such as is suffered, for example, by children who witness domestic violence. It would be a mistake to assume that the increasing recognition of child abuse as a major social problem reflected any change in its incidence. Rather, the increased visibility of child abuse that we have seen over the past three decades reflects new social choices and priorities. Sociologists therefore talk about the *social construction* of child abuse as a social problem, seeming to demand particular solutions and the involvement of particular welfare experts.

THE CLEVELAND CRISIS: PARENTS OF LEEDS CHILDREN DEMONSTRATE THEIR FEELINGS OUTSIDE MIDDLESBROUGH TOWN HALL.

DEFINING CHILD ABUSE

A sociologist wishing to define child abuse is faced with the same sorts of problems that beset one interested in domestic violence; precise definitions that can be agreed upon by everyone are difficult to reach. Defining concepts, particularly one as emotive as child abuse, necessarily involves making subjective judgements and invoking values about what behaviours we think are 'normal' and acceptable, and what we decide requires intervention or punishment. The study of child abuse is necessarily an imprecise science. But definitions are important; if we don't know what the problem is that we are talking about, how can we find out anything about its causes or its incidence?

In general terms, child abuse can be defined as anything that adversely interferes with children's basic human rights or their development. As our conceptions of children, of their rights and of their developmental needs and requirements necessarily change over time and from culture to culture, it follows that what is regarded as 'abuse' is similarly fluid and contingent. Thus, as stated above, in our own society, the category of 'abuse' has expanded over the last thirty years or so. The Children Act 1989 guidelines mention four specific categories of abuse and provide some definition for each: neglect, physical injury, sexual abuse and emotional abuse. As with domestic violence, the incidence of child abuse is impossible to estimate with any degree of accuracy. Obviously, any estimates of incidence will depend very heavily upon how abuse is defined.

Study point
Why is it difficult to define child abuse and to find out about its incidence?

EXPLAINING CHILD ABUSE

There are five main explanatory models that have been proposed. We will briefly discuss each in turn. It is important, however, to bear in mind that because there is no single category of abuse, any one explanation is likely to be insufficient. Furthermore, the ways in which we seek to make sense of abuse necessarily reflect ideologies and cultural values, which themselves are not static, but shifting.

People who abuse children are not 'normal'. This model is really a psychological one. It suggests that the perpetrators of abuse are abnormal in some way, sick or criminal. The model predicts that there will be significant differences between those who abuse children and those who don't. However, this is not supported by the evidence; psychologists have failed to find a consistent personality profile that distinguishes people who abuse children as a specific category of people.

The 'cycle of violence'. This model is currently a popular one and is often invoked in social work practice. It suggests that people become abusers because they were abused themselves as children. The model accounts for the ways in which abuse can be passed from one generation to the next. However, as sociologists have pointed out, the model is not adequately supported by the evidence. Clearly, some abusers have themselves been victims, but this is by no means true of all abusers and, importantly, there are many adults who were abused as children who do not go on to repeat the process with their own children. Moreover, whilst it is true that childhood experiences are likely to affect one's adult self, no straightforward causal mechanisms can be identified that could justify explaining abuse in terms of a cycle of violence. Contemporary sociologists prefer to see people as meaning–making animals, and point out that they are active agents who weigh things up and make choices of their own; they are not just the passive recipients of things that have been done to them in childhood. Therefore, although the 'cycle of violence' model is popularly employed in common–sense thinking there is little evidential support for it, and the assumptions upon which it is based are matters of some debate in sociology.

Child abuse is the result of a dysfunctional family system. This model sees the abuse of one child as connected to the broader set of family relationships, where the family is viewed as a 'system' with particular habitual patterns of beliefs, interactions and communication. On this view, each family member plays a specific part in the maintenance of the family system. Child abuse is symptomatic of a *dysfunctional* family system, that requires expert interventions, and welfare work with the whole family, to address the problem. The main criticism that sociologists have levelled against this model is that it presupposes a particular kind of functional, *normal* family, which reflects prevailing ideologies about gender roles. For example, the wives of men who sexually abuse children have been regarded as colluding in the abuse by failing to satisfy their husbands' sexual needs. The responsibility for the abuse is not placed with the abuser, but is seen as the responsibility of the whole family, including the victims themselves. Recently, the 'systems' model has been refined by psycho–dynamically informed therapists who have some sympathy with the sociological viewpoint, and there is an increasing emphasis in practice on the importance of the abuser acknowledging responsibility for what they have done before serious therapeutic work can start.

Child abuse is a result of adverse social circumstances. This model suggests that the stresses incurred in situations of prolonged adversity, such as illness, unemployment or poverty, can lead to increased frustration and anger; people lose control of themselves and hurt their children, as the weakest, most vulnerable members of the family. The model acknowledges that ongoing frustrations and feelings of powerlessness can lead to lapses in rational behaviour, and to angry or violent outbursts. Clearly this model cannot account for all cases of abuse, many of which show systematic abuse that is not compatible with the idea of having reached the end of one's tether in a moment of stress. In addition, there are many families who suffer prolonged stresses of one sort and another, but they do not go on to abuse their children.

Child abuse is related to social structures and cultural ideologies. This is the model favoured by feminist sociologists. It suggests that, like domestic violence, child abuse is the result of unequal power within the family; both women and children are rendered vulnerable to male abuse and violence by the positions accorded them by society. On this view, child abuse, like domestic violence, is an abuse of male power. It is important to note, as Segal has done, that dominant ideologies of masculinity continue to emphasise domination and control. Also, as Kitzinger argues, our society tends to construct children as vulnerable and dependent. Child abuse is therefore seen as a problem that arises due to the ways in which society habitually conceives of adults and children; it permits adults, in many circumstances to dominate children and to make decisions on their behalf, on the grounds that children are not sufficiently competent to do some things for themselves. It is but a small step, says Kitzinger, towards using excessive physical force or sexual violence to impose our will on children. This model therefore places social ideologies and gendered practices at the forefront in its attempt to understand child abuse.

Study point
Suggest some reasons why men seem to abuse children more often than women do.

ADDRESSING THE PROBLEM OF CHILD ABUSE

Each of the explanatory models we have discussed has different implications for what should be done about the problem of child abuse. Individual and family therapies, of various kinds, have proliferated in recent years, and some abusive men who are sent to prison have been obliged to participate in educational and therapeutic programmes, with varying results. Governments could tackle issues of stresses on families caused by poverty and the increasingly uncertain world of employment, but to date no noticeable difference has been made. Social workers continue to administer the 'child protection' system, attempting to identify children who are 'at risk' and either to provide support for families or to initiate care proceedings that result in the removal of children from their families into foster homes and children's homes.

Activity
List five explanatory models that have been proposed to account for child abuse. Which do you think is the most plausible, and why?

Ironically perhaps, in recent years we have witnessed widespread criticism of the child protection system; children who were actually abused whilst 'in care' are now going public about their experiences, and the media has given wide coverage to their stories. Feminist sociologists would argue that the problem of child abuse will be unlikely to be alleviated until society has rid itself of patriarchal structures and ideologies, and has empowered children as a social group and recognised their rights to full citizenship. They would see the child protection system as part of the problem of child abuse, rather than being its solution, as social work rhetoric and practice perpetuate notions of children as powerless and in need of protection.

Activity

Why does Kitzinger propose that child protection systems are part of the problem of child abuse and not its solution?

SUMMARY

In recent years both domestic violence and child abuse have emerged as major social problems, demanding attention. The existence of such problems has cast doubt on Functionalist assumptions that families are functional and that they provide safe havens for people. Critics of the Functionalist school have argued that domestic violence and child abuse indicate the dysfunctional nature of many families. Both domestic violence and child abuse are notoriously hard to define. As they occur within the 'private' confines of the home, their incidence is also difficult to estimate.

Four main models have been proposed in an attempt to understand why domestic violence occurs. The first model is a biological one, assuming that male violence is innate, natural and instinctive. The main problem with this model is that human beings are mammals, but they are not just animals; human society and culture, at the very least, mediates biological givens, and human behaviours have meaning in cultural contexts. The second model proposes that individual abusers are pathological in some way. This may well be so in some cases but, if this model were to hold good in *all* cases, we would have to accept that a substantial minority of men are 'abnormal'. The third model sees the interactions between partners as the cause of violence. It may be that some people have communication patterns that are far from the ideals of mutual tolerance and respect, but this model cannot explain the gendered dimension of the problem of domestic violence — why it is that the vast majority of abusers are men and the vast majority of victims are women. From a therapeutic standpoint also, this model can amount to 'victim–blaming' — it fails to oblige individual abusers to take responsibility for what they have done. The fourth model proposes that domestic violence reflects gendered power differences that pervade 'normal' society. This is the model favoured by feminist sociologists. It suggests that domestic violence is a social problem engendered by valued forms of masculinity and femininity in our culture; the use of force becomes an extreme manifestation of men's desire to subjugate women. On this model, all men are potential abusers and all women are their potential victims. The main problems with this model are twofold: It fails to explain why individual incidents of violence occur when they do, and it does not account for the violence that is sometimes found in homosexual partnerships.

Five main models have been proposed to explain child abuse. First, the idea that abusers are abnormal in some way is widely accepted. Yet, it has not been possible for psychologists to find a distinct personality profile that distinguishes those who abuse from those who don't. The second model proposes that abused children are more likely to become abusers themselves in adulthood, thus setting up a 'cycle of violence'. There are a lot of problems with this model, not least that it takes little account of human agency and meaning. The third model proposes that abuse is the result of a dysfunctional family system, but this model, in its less sophisticated forms, fails to place responsibility for the abuse on the abuser. Child abuse has also been thought to be related to the stress occasioned by adverse social circumstances, but there are many families who live with prolonged stress and adversity and whose interactions remain healthy nevertheless. The final model proposes that child abuse cannot be separated from social structures and cultural ideologies, and the powerless position of children in relation to adults is cited as an important factor. This model, however, cannot explain individual instances of abuse.

STUDY GUIDES

Group activities

1 Write to the *Women's Aid Federation for England* and find out about the work that they do. Are they supported by government funds? Find out about whether there are any other voluntary organisations to help women who are abused by their partners. What is the scope of their work? In your group, put together a dossier of the sources of help that are available.

2 Ask someone from your local social services department to come to your school or college to explain how they deal with cases of suspected child abuse.

3 Work together to critically evaluate the 'cycle of violence' model of child abuse.

Practice questions

Item A

Work by feminist activists and researchers has produced strong evidence that the roots of domestic violence lie not in pathology, stress or family conflicts but in men's domination and control over women ... The abusive behaviours characteristic of men in violent relationships are best described as control tactics, ways of instilling fear and coercing compliance. These tactics are part of the language of the relationship which women become highly skilled at interpreting. Violent men often give out very subtle, verbal and non–verbal, signals of their threats and intentions — signals which would be unrecognisable to anyone except those they are abusing. Behaviours not obviously abusive to an outsider can signal extreme danger to the woman on the receiving end, and hence terrorise her; indeed, violence does not have to be continuous or physical for her to be terrified that she could be harmed at any moment. A lack of understanding of these features of violent relationships, along with the difficulties women have in naming and/or disclosing the violence ... may partly explain why professionals often underestimate or disregard the seriousness of the situation, to the detriment of women's and children's safety.

Audrey Mullender and Rebecca Morley, 1994, *Children Living With Domestic Violence*, Whiting and Birch, p7.

Item B

[We examine] recent and contradictory developments which have taken place in Britain with regard to women, violence from known men and child contact. That is, how legislation and professional practice in relation to domestic violence — seeking to protect women against violence from male partners — is being undermined through the impact of the Children Act 1989, which focuses on contact between children and parents after parents separate or divorce. On the one hand there has been increasing recognition by the State, in terms of legislation and law enforcement, of the need for intervention where men are being violent to female partners. This has resulted in the, albeit limited, development and growth of some positive approaches to facilitating women's safety. Since the late 1980s the police in particular have claimed to be changing their attitudes and have introduced some useful initiatives. On the other hand, the new legislation on child care, which also concerns separating parents and their children, the Children Act, has tended to affect women's safety negatively. Specifically, professionals working in this area of family law are misinterpreting child welfare in contact cases. A child's 'right to know' a parent and to have contact with him or her is taking precedence over considerations for the mother's safety as well as the child's safety and well–being through contact with the violent father.

Marianne Hester and Lorraine Radford, 1996, 'Contradictions and compromises: the impact of the Children Act on women's and children's safety', in M. Hester et al (eds.) *Women, Violence and Male Power*, Open University Press, p81.

Item C

Most of us are now familiar with the images of childhood associated with discussions of child sexual abuse on TV, in newspapers and in child protection leaflets. The abused child is represented by an anonymous figure sitting limp and despairing with her head in her hands, or by the brother and sister gazing wistfully from behind a window, or, sometimes, simply by a broken doll. These images can be objectifying and voyeuristic in themselves but, however 'tasteful', they invariably emphasise the child's youth and passivity. When particular cases are documented, the pen–portraits of the victim always focus on child–specific attributes such as pig–tails, hair ribbons, her sailor–suit dress, her 'favourite plastic purse with the rainbow handles' or her Paddington Bear clock ... Even 'serious investigative journalism' documenting children's sexual exploitation, may employ, as background music, the tinkling sound of a musical box ... All these props accentuate the fact that the victim is a child — childhood itself is an issue; in case we are in any doubt, the sexual abuse of a child is often referred to as 'the theft or violation of childhood' ... Implicit, then, in all such documentation is an assertion of what childhood 'really is'. Childhood is presented as a time of play, an asexual and peaceful existence within the protective bosom of the family. This image is both ethnocentric and unrealistic.

Jenny Kitzinger, 1988, 'Defending innocence: ideologies of childhood', in *Feminist Review*, No. 28, Special Issue on Child Sexual Abuse, pp77–78.

1 With reference to Item A and elsewhere, critically evaluate the idea that domestic violence is best explained in terms of gendered power relationships. What other models have been proposed to explain men's violence against their female partners?
2 With reference to Item B, suggest a way in which the problem referred to could be effectively addressed by Family Law.
3 With reference to Item C, explain why you think the author sees this particular construction of childhood as a problem in relation to child sexual abuse.
4 With reference to elsewhere, list five models that have been proposed to explain child abuse.
5 With reference to elsewhere, give two reasons why the incidence of child abuse is difficult to estimate.

Coursework suggestions

1 Write an essay in which you describe and critically evaluate THREE models for the causes of domestic violence. Say which model you prefer, and why. What are the implications of your preferred model for tackling the problem?
2 Write an essay in which you describe and critically evaluate THREE models for the causes of child abuse. Say which model you prefer, and why. What are the implications of your preferred model for tackling the problem?
3 Write a review of Alice Walker's novel *The Colour Purple*.
4 Write a review of Roddy Doyle's novel *The Woman Who Walked Into Doors*.

9

FAMILIES AND THE STATE

Introduction

SOCIOLOGISTS HAVE LONG deliberated about the relationship between the family and the State. As we have seen, families are *both* social institutions *and* sites for our closest, most intimate relationships. As stable, functional families are seen as central to social cohesion and prosperity, the State has an interest in promoting particular kinds of values and behaviours. Yet, in democratic societies, it cannot go too far, and a balance must be drawn between the interventions that are strictly necessary (as for example in cases of child abuse) and the need to safeguard individual rights and freedom from unwarranted state intrusion into our private intimate lives. The balance is not an easy one to draw, and sociologists would argue that there is a fine line between state *support* for families and *social engineering* or control.

Table 10: *Key theorists, concepts and issues*		
KEY THEORISTS	KEY CONCEPTS	KEY ISSUES
C. Lasch	The State	Does the State support or undermine the family?
F. Mount	State support for families	Does Britain have a family policy?
J. Donzelot	Social engineering	Should Britain have a family policy?
	Social control	
	Public/private dualism	
	Welfare State	
	Family Law	
	Family policy	

The main sociological debate has been about whether the State, particularly the *Welfare State*, either supports or threatens the family. A closely associated issue is whether the family is accurately portrayed as a *private* sphere that is fundamentally separate from the *public* world of work, the economy, law and the State. These issues continue to cause intense debate in sociology and, as we will see, there is no easy answer to the question of the relation between family and state.

One reason for the difficulty in arriving at a plain and simple resolution to the debate is that neither *the* family nor *the* State can be conceived of in simple terms, as monolithic entities. In chapter 2, we discussed the difficulties inherent in arriving at a single consensus around the meaning of 'family', and we pointed out that the term 'families', in the plural, more accurately captures the contemporary diversity and fluid nature of family forms. Similar points can be made in relation to 'the State'.

Our modern *Welfare State* grew up in Britain in the years after the Second World War. It embodied priorities of fairness and equality and, importantly, support for family life was at the heart of the post–war reconstruction programme. This was what Goldthorpe called the 'golden age' of the nuclear family. At a time when the family was seen as the cornerstone of society and as the main guarantor of social stability, the focus of the Welfare State on rebuilding family and society together, after the ravages of war, is entirely understandable. The government of the day introduced new health care provisions and family allowances (now called 'child benefit'), it instituted an extensive programme of public housing, and put in place a range of other welfare provisions all designed to provide support for families as a way of rebuilding society after the War. Since then, the Welfare State has undergone many changes, but it has always had multiple dimensions. The Welfare State cannot be considered to be a single entity, but instead consists of a variety of institutions and agencies, all with different briefs and different priorities, and all competing for a share of the public purse.

Laws and policies in one area of the State (for example, social welfare provision) have not always gone hand in hand with those in another, and the range of things that can be done is always constrained by the funds available and successive Chancellors' willingness to spend it. Thus, we necessarily have a situation where welfare ideologies can sometimes be out of kilter with practices, or policies and practices at odds with each other. There may not always be the money available to implement sorely needed policy changes. The effects of some policies may undermine or even contradict the objectives of others, and the outcomes of policy provisions do not necessarily reflect what was envisaged as their original purpose.

Nowhere are these problems more evident than in divorce policy. Successive reforms of the law on divorce, according to Ruth Deech, often seem to have had the opposite effects from those intended by the policy makers. Rather than supporting marriage and stemming the tide of divorce, reforms in recent years have been followed by an apparently ever–increasing divorce rate. As we also noted, in connection with the Children Act, the policy aims of encouraging fathers to maintain responsibility for children and providing for the more peaceful resolution of divorce disputes, have not been realised in practice; in fact, the opposite seems to be happening.

Thus, sociologists recognise that to talk about *the* State as a unitary entity, or to equate the effects of policies with their avowed aims, is as erroneous as imagining that *the* family exists in any unequivocal way. The complexities of family forms and relationships, and of public policies, are likely to pose obstacles to the straightforward resolution of sociological debates about state–family relations. Of course, it can be argued that the purpose of sociological debates is not to find easy answers, but rather is to deepen our understanding of the complexities of social life, and to help us decide which of our theories best fits the facts and the evidence. In this chapter, we explore the sociological debate about the relationship between the family and the State. We look at both sides of the debate, examining first the arguments that the State supports the family and then the contrary view, that the family is threatened or undermined by the State.

THE STATE SUPPORTS THE FAMILY

The idea that the State supports the family is the dominant position in contemporary government rhetoric and underlies, for example, the practices of welfare professionals such as mental health workers, health visitors, and social workers. When Mrs Thatcher was Prime Minister, there began a concerted programme of 'liberating' the family from state intrusions and of restoring to citizens responsibility for their own lives. This was part and parcel of Mrs Thatcher's particular interpretation of *laissez-faire* capitalist democracy. Great emphasis was placed on the 'rolling back' of the State to give individuals and families 'freedom to choose' how to run their own lives, away from the constraints of the 'nanny' State. The desire to reduce poorer families' dependence upon state help, and the expectation that they should take responsibility for themselves, and rely on their own resources was, of course, the other side of the same coin.

The Conservative Government of 1979–1997 presided over both the Children Act as well as a major reform of the divorce law, designed to reduce the role of lawyers and courts in the divorce process, and to encourage parents to reach their own agreements about their post–divorce arrangements. These changes were portrayed as providing support for families and of restoring to them some semblance of privacy and autonomy. Sociologists, however, looked beyond the rhetoric of 'freedom' and 'choice' and saw, instead, that a fundamental change in the Welfare State was underway, a change that reduced the entitlement of poor and vulnerable groups to services and resources that could guarantee their basic rights as citizens.

Activity

List as many state supports for families (e.g. Child Benefit) as you can think of.

But the ideology that accompanied the changes in welfare provision under the Thatcher and Major Governments was a powerful one, and its legacy in New Labour's welfare agenda is evident. The idea that the State supports the family remains a dominant one. On this view, the State, through a range of agencies, supports the family in the performance of its essential functions by providing both material assistance (such as financial help to families in need) and services (such as, for example, education and social work). It is argued that such state assistance has the effect of helping families to perform the functions required of them. At the same time, families are discouraged from expecting too much or becoming too dependent upon what the State provides.

Importantly, Britain has never had a 'family policy' as such. Other social policies, such as those around taxation, social security, housing, and family law, obviously impact on families, for better or worse, but there has never been an attempt to co–ordinate and integrate the various provisions in a 'family policy'. We may shortly witness some change in this respect as New Labour has declared its intention to provide a coherent family policy and in 1998 they issued a consultation paper *Supporting Families* to begin the debate about what governments can best do to support families. The proposals for family policy focus on parents and their dependent children (and not, for example, on the elderly) and indicate that the Government regards marriage as the preferred basis for family life and for the raising of children.

As we have seen in previous chapters, however, this emphasis on marriage flies in the face of changes in the patterns of partnering and parenting, and in expectations associated with intimacy. In fact, increasing numbers of people are choosing not to marry, and increasing numbers of children are born outside of formal marriage. The Government has been at pains not to ignore these changes, or to appear to undermine the work that many non–traditional families do and the undoubted successes they can achieve. However, at the same time, it is true to say that the rhetoric of successive governments has been in support of 'traditional' or nuclear families, based on marriage. This sits uneasily with the emphasis on freedom of choice and the avowed respect for those who choose not to opt for marriage.

Successive legal reforms around, for example, divorce, child abuse and domestic violence can also be seen as providing some evidence for the idea that the State supports the family. These reforms indicate that law and policy can, and do, acknowledge the realities of social change and can adapt to meet changing needs, meanings and expectations of family life.

Activity

Discuss what you think the benefits might be if Britain adopts a family policy. Can you think of some potential disadvantages?

However, family policies both *respond* to and *direct* social change. They are perhaps best regarded as being engaged in the service of drawing and re–drawing the delicate balance between, on the one hand, maintaining family privacy from unwarranted state intrusions and, on the other hand, providing support for weaker and more vulnerable family members, such as children. The balance, however, is a difficult one to draw, and inevitably will not please everyone.

Activity

Summarise in a short paragraph the main points of the argument that the State supports the family.

THE STATE THREATENS THE FAMILY

Claims that the State is introducing measures to support the family are apt to be challenged by critics who allege that the very same policies are actually undermining the family and robbing it of its functions, its privacy or its autonomy. The argument that the family is threatened by the State has its origins in Functionalist sociology (see chapter 3). The Functionalist position was that, with the advent of industrialisation, the State increasingly took over what had previously been some of the functions of the family (for example, production and education) with the result that the functions of the family became more limited and specialised (for example, the socialisation of children, and emotional support for family members). This tendency, it is argued, has become more pronounced with the growth of the modern Welfare State.

Pessimistic Functionalists expressed the fear that the public state was intruding in the private world of the family and undermining it by progressively taking over its functions. For example, Ferdinand Mount, in his book *The Subversive Family* (1982) argued that the private world of the family was increasingly being eroded by state intrusions. He saw the family as the last bastion against Orwellian 1984–style, 'big brother' state control of people's private lives. For him, the privacy and integrity of the family were the best guarantors of resistance to collectivist ideologies and the expansion of socialist policies.

Activity
Discuss why you think Ferdinand Mount called his book *The Subversive Family*.

In a similar way, Christopher Lasch in his *Haven in a Heartless World* (1977) showed how the process of industrialisation was accompanied by the growth of the capitalist state. Part and parcel of this development was the growth of an army of welfare experts, whose ideologies and practices were supported by scientific theories, and whose sole purpose it was to manage the private lives of citizens. As a result, he said, our private lives have become increasingly open to public scrutiny, and the family as a private sphere has been undermined.

Study point
What assumptions are embedded in the idea that the family is a 'haven in a heartless world'?

Summarise in a short paragraph the argument that the State threatens the family.

BEYOND THE DEBATE

French sociologist Jaques Donzelot, working within a *post–structuralist* framework, goes further than most theorists in this debate. His work points to the conclusion that the whole question of whether the State supports the family, or whether it does the opposite, is something of a red herring. He points out that 'the family' is a fluid concept, a shifting set of practices and relationships, that is ideologically constructed as a 'private' sphere but which is, in fact, 'public' at its core. His work therefore actively challenges the public/private division that has informed much sociological debate on the family. He maintains that this old dualism is itself a product of capitalist ideology, and has to be transcended if we are to understand the nature of the family and its relationship to the State. For him, 'the family' is very much a product of social, political and economic forces. As such, it cannot simply be characterised as a 'private' sphere and, in any event, what we think of as the private sphere is itself ideologically constructed.

Donzelot's view, as set out in his book *The Policing of Families* (1980) is therefore rather more complex (and challenging to the reader!) than that of most other work in family sociology. His work is located in a French tradition of post–structuralist philosophy and sociology, and his ideas can be difficult to grasp. In many ways, they challenge our traditional ways of thinking but, in so doing, they remind us of the ideologies that are embedded in our own world–views and in our common–sense concepts. Donzelot's ideas make sense if we can put aside, for the moment, our own habitual modes of thought that are heavily influenced by prevailing ideologies.

What is the significance of Donzelot's point that the family is ideologically constructed as 'private' sphere, but is actually 'public' at its core?

They make sense if we think, for example, about the role played by family law and public policy in influencing how we think, and how we feel, about families. Laws and policies do not simply *reflect* what a society thinks about a particular issue but, in important ways, they present to us images about what families *should* be doing and what they *should* be like. Sociologists such as Carol Smart refer to this as *social engineering*, and see it as an attempt, by the State, to engineer social change in a particular direction.

Currently, for example, we are witnessing a high premium placed on marriage and on so-called 'traditional' families. If we reflect, for a moment, on our own experience of families, we become aware that families are less *natural groupings* than they are *social arrangements*, often supported by laws and constrained by other policy provisions.

Points of evaluation

- Laws, such as those governing marriage, divorce, adoption, and so on, actually provide a bedrock for defining *what families are* and *who family members are*, and who is entitled to do what to whom with impunity.
- Laws of succession (that govern what happens to a person's property when they die); provisions for social security entitlement, pension rights and provisions for the transfer of tenancies; policies for taxation and the right to take matters concerning children to court, and so on, are all built around very particular notions of what family is, and who is entitled to claim the status of family or kin group membership.
- This means that, from the start, the State plays a part in bringing families into being and maintaining them by according them status as legal entities. In the light of these arguments, the idea that family and state are in any sense independent of each other, or that the public and the private are separable, is simply not tenable. This is Donzelot's point.

The Power of Familial Ideologies

Donzelot argues that in late–modern industrialised societies, a rhetoric of freedom and choice is underpinned by a less than obvious mode of social control, based on welfare. The government of citizens, he says, is increasingly achieved *through* families, as welfare policies embody ideas about what families *should* be like, what kind of relationships between family members are right and proper, what practices are likely to foster optimal child development, and so on. These implicit ideas inform not only what people may legitimately *do* in families, but also what they *think* and *feel*, and what they aspire to achieve in family settings. Based on this argument, the social control of citizens by the state is largely dependent upon welfare policies, and the associated expert practices that are directed at families, rather than at individuals. For example, child protection policies, implemented by the social work profession in relation to children 'at risk', embody implicit ideas about what it takes to be a 'good' parent as well as particular visions of childhood (see chapter 8).

Thus Donzelot characterises the workings of a set of policies and practices around the family as constituting a *policing* of families by the State. This is an important idea, because it cuts across the old public/private divide, and suggests that the question of whether the State supports or undermines the family, which has provoked so much debate, is too naïve a formulation and may, in fact, be something of a red herring. The State and the family are mutually dependent, and the family is neither undermined nor supported by the State. Rather, it is a social institution that is both created and maintained by ideologies, policies and welfare practices.

This new formulation is currently enjoying much popularity in sociology. Importantly, it allows for state–family relationships to be conceived in reciprocal terms, and permits some conceptualisation of the influence that families may have on the State; the relationship is very much a two–way process. Changes in mentalities around intimacy, such as those discussed by Giddens (see chapter 6), and changes in family forms and patterns (see chapter 1), themselves exert an influence on public policy in a two–way process.

The old Functionalist ideas that prioritised the impact of the State upon the family generally failed to accord families, and family members, any agency or autonomy in the process. Functionalist theories were widely criticised for their implicit portrayal of human citizens as the passive recipients of social forces. By contrast, the more recent sociological ideas that we have outlined above permit a more complex and nuanced conception of state–family relations, as a two–way process that permits some consideration of the contributions made by active human subjects to living their lives in families in an ever–evolving relationship with other social institutions.

In our discussion, we have not resolved the debate about whether the State supports or undermines the family. Rather, we have used sociological ideas to shift the terrain of the debate and have indicated that the answers one can provide to the question depend very much upon how one reads the evidence, and the theoretical frameworks one invokes to inform understanding. Sociology is a critical discipline, and if we are to learn to be good sociologists, it is important that we learn to question, not only the evidence, but also the terms and premises of sociological debates.

Points of Evaluation
- In conclusion, it can be said that the State neither supports nor undermines the family, because there is no single 'state' that we can identify and no single 'family' that it can act upon.
- On the other hand, it may also be said that the State supports the family in some ways, and undermines it in others.
- Overall, family laws and welfare policies do seem to support a particular middle–class ideology of the private, white, nuclear family, with its segregated gender roles and dependent, vulnerable children. Feminist sociologists, as we saw in chapter 4, have identified the dominance of this particular ideology in the face of realities that are somewhat different, as evidence of the continuance of patriarchal values in our culture.

- Yet, on the other hand, we do not have to look far to discover instances where state policies provide some kind of support for weaker members of the community. Instances of domestic violence, child abuse and rape within marriage are cases in point. Rape within marriage was recognised as a criminal offence in 1991; before that, many women were at risk of sexual assault by their partners by virtue of the simple fact of marriage. In recent years, the law has done much to improve the situation for women abused by their partners ('battered women') and to provide new legal remedies to protect them and their children. However, some would argue that the current provisions do not go far enough, and that state responses to problems such as family violence are inevitably constrained by the implicit ideologies about gender roles, about how families should be and about the sanctity of marriage.

Summary Points
1 In summary, it may be that if the State supports anything it is not real families, in all their diversity, but instead is a particular ideal — that of the nuclear family based on marriage. We regularly hear, in the media and in the speeches of politicians, about families that depart from this ideal, and are denigrated and blamed for other social problems, such as juvenile crime.
2 At the same time, statistics tell us that lone–parent families are amongst the poorest in society. These families have real needs that could be alleviated by measures provided by the State. These families clearly lack the support of the State. It would seem that the State supports the ideal of the family, but not the realities of most families.

SUMMARY

The issue of the relationship between the family and the State has provoked much sociological debate. In democratic societies, families have traditionally been seen as private institutions that should, as far as possible, remain free from state intervention and control; the 'private' and the 'public' are seen as separate spheres. The balance between safeguarding citizens' rights to freedom and intervening to protect the vulnerable, has always been a difficult one to draw. Thus there is always a fine line between state 'support' for families, and social engineering and control.

The main sociological debate has been about whether the State, particularly the Welfare State, either supports or undermines the family. The question has not been easy to resolve, not least because 'the State', like 'the family' is not a monolithic entity.

Those who argue that the State supports the family point to the range of government agencies and initiatives that provide support by way of services and financial help for families in need. Those who argue that the State threatens the family see such support as an intrusion that compromises the privacy of the family and takes over some of its functions.

Sociologists working in the post–structuralist tradition have made an important contribution to this difficult debate. They argue that families are a product of social forces and that they therefore necessarily have a 'public' dimension. In all sorts of ways, the State constructs the family, and so there can be no rigid separation between the two. On this view, the dichotomies of family/state and private/public are ideologies that serve to maintain the myth that families are relatively independent of the State. This perspective does not so much resolve the debate as alter its terms. It generates new questions; instead of asking whether the State supports or undermines the family, the question becomes one of how the governance of citizens in democratic societies is achieved.

STUDY GUIDES

Group activities

1 Find the Government document 'Supporting Families' using the Internet (Home Office web site — a copy can also be obtained from the Home Office if you cannot access it on the web site). Discuss in your group whether the proposed 'supports' for families will be helpful, or whether they amount to unwarranted interference in family life.

2 Using the 'Supporting Families' document, discuss in your group whether, in your view, the Government's proposals adequately respect non–traditional family forms.

3 Conduct a class debate: This house believes that the State could do more to support the family.

Item A

As I hope I made clear, we have high ambitions for this Bill. We hope and believe that it will bring order, integration, relevance and a better balance to the law — a better balance not just between the rights and responsibilities of individuals and agencies, but, most vitally, between the need to protect children and the need to enable parents to challenge intervention in the upbringing of their children.

David Mellor, Minister of State at the Department of Health, speaking in the House of Commons on 27 April 1989, on the public law provisions of the Children Bill (which later became the Children Act, 1989). *Hansard*, HoC, Vol. 151, No. 94, Col.1107.

Item B

State–family interaction is never likely to be free of an element of coercion where state welfare is provided, because of the contested — and shifting — boundary between state and family responsibility and the State's incentive to get the family to do more. There is an ideological divide between left and right here, with the right much more insistent than the left on the responsibility of family members for dependency. This area of ambiguity applies to cash income from the State versus maintenance by a relative, and to other kinds of care and help, and indeed to some extent to education and socialisation. Examples of contested and shifting boundaries, where both state and family are recognised as having some (but an unclear) degree of responsibility, would be the social care of the elderly, the care of children outside school … child socialisation and sex education. Where family responsibilities are not 'properly' met, a number of state responses may come into play. These range from deploying punitive sanctions against family members (including the use of the criminal law, for example, to punish parents for their children's offences, or prosecutions for non–maintenance of dependants), through the removal of dependent individuals from the family … through deductions for maintenance from wages or benefits, to abandoning state responsibility on the assumption that family members will meet *their* responsibilities (which sometimes means leaving dependent persons vulnerable to neglect, destitution, homelessness, and so on).

Lorraine Fox Harding, 1996, *Family State and Social Policy*, Macmillan, p108.

1 With reference to Item A and elsewhere, decide whether you think the 'balance' referred to is tipped in favour of families, or of the State, in relation to child abuse. Give reasons for your decision.

2 With reference to Item B, explain what the author means by the 'shifting boundary' between the family and the State.

3 With reference to Item B, assess how compatible the existence of punitive sanctions are with the ideology of the family as a 'private' sphere.

4 With reference to elsewhere, give three examples to show that state policies in relation to the family can justifiably be described as 'social engineering'.

5 With reference to elsewhere, give three examples of state 'support' for families.

Coursework suggestions

1 Critically evaluate the argument that state policies since the Second World War have undermined the family and robbed it of its functions.

2 Critically evaluate the argument that the State supports the family.

3 Do some research to collect information about the range of welfare services that currently exist, and make an annotated scrap book.

FURTHER READING AND RESOURCES

GENERAL TEXTS

Bernardes, J. (1997) *Family Studies: An Introduction*. Routledge, London.

Giddens, A. (1989) *Sociology*. Polity, Cambridge. (Chapter 12)

Macionis, J. and Plummer, K. (1998) *Sociology*. Prentice Hall, London. (Chapter 17)

Morgan, D.H.J. (1996) *Family Connections*. Polity, Cambridge.

Rapaport, R.N., Fogarty, M. and Rapaport, R. (eds) (1982) *Families in Britain*. Routledge and Kegan Paul, London.

Family Studies Abstracts, published by Sage, gives up–to–date summaries of recent research.

READERS

Allen, G. (ed.) (1999) *The Sociology of the Family; A Reader*. Blackwell, Oxford.

Fox, B. (ed.) (1993) *Family Patterns, Gender Relations*. Oxford University Press, Oxford.

Muncie, J., Wetherell, M., Dallos, R. and Cochrane, A. (eds.) (1995) *Understanding the Family*. Sage, London (second, revised edition, 1999).

WHAT IS 'THE FAMILY'?

Abbott, P. and Wallace, C. (1992) *The Family and the New Right*. Pluto, London.

Coote, A., Harman, H. and Hewitt, H. (1994) 'Changing patterns of family life', in J. Eekelaar and M. Maclean (eds) *A Reader on Family Law*. Oxford University Press, Oxford.

Gittins, D. (1993) *The Family in Question: Changing Households and Familiar Ideologies*. Macmillan, Basingstoke.

Hubbard, R. (1995) *Family Change Database*, Family Policy Studies Centre, London (for address, see below).

Scott, J. (1997) 'Changing households in Britain: do families still matter?', in *The Sociological Review*, vol.45, No.4, pp.591–620.

Silva, E. and Smart, C. (eds) (1999) *The New Family?* Sage, London.

Official publications from the *Office for National Statistics* and *Social Trends* give periodical data on demographic change.

FUNCTIONALISM AND ITS CRITICS

Abbott, P. and Wallace, C. (1997) *An Introduction to Sociology: Feminist Perspectives*. Routledge, London. (Chapter 6 on The Family and the Household)

Anderson, M. (ed.) (1980) *Sociology of the Family: Selected Readings*. Penguin, Harmondsworth.

Elliott, F.R. (1986) *The Family: Change or Continuity?* Macmillan, Basingstoke.

Fletcher, R. (1966) *The Family and Marriage in Britain*. Pelican, Harmondsworth.

Parsons, T. and Bales, R.F. (1955) *Family Socialisation and Interaction Process*. Glencoe, Free Press.

Young, M. and Wilmott, P. (1957) *Family and Kinship in East London*. Pelican, Harmondsworth.

Young, M. and Wilmott, P. (1973) *The Symmetrical Family*. Penguin, Harmondsworth.

Zaretsky, E. (1976) *Capitalism, the Family and Personal Life*, Pluto, London.

HISTORICAL PERSPECTIVES

Anderson, M. (1980) *Approaches to the History of the Western Family*. Cambridge University Press, Cambridge.

Drake, M. (ed.) (1994) *Time, Family and Community*. Blackwell, Oxford.

Laslett, P. (1979) *The World We Have Lost*. Methuen, London.

Seccombe, W. (1992) *A Millennium of Family Change*. Verso, London.

Stone, L. (1977) *The Family, Sex and Marriage in England 1500–1800*. Pelican, Harmondsworth.

DIFFERENCE AND DIVERSITY

Dallos, R. and Sapsford, R. (1995) 'Patterns of Diversity and Lived Realities', in R. Dallos *et al* (eds) *Understanding the Family*. Sage, London.

Dunne, G. (1997) *Lesbian Lifestyles: Women's Work and the Politics of Sexuality*. Macmillan, Basingstoke.

Elliott, F.R. (1996) *Gender, Family and Society*. Macmillan, Basingstoke.

Haskey, J. (1989) 'Families and households of the ethnic minority and white populations of Great Britain', *Population Trends*, vol. 57, pp.8–19.

Oakley, J. (1983) *The Traveller Gypsies*. Cambridge University Press, Cambridge.

Sibley, D. (1981) *Outsiders in Urban Societies*. Blackwell, Oxford.

INTIMACY, COHABITATION, MARRIAGE AND DIVORCE

Day Sclater, S. and Piper, C. (1999) *Undercurrents of Divorce*. Ashgate, Aldershot.

Donnellan, C. (ed.) (1996) *Marriage and Divorce: Issues for the Nineties*. Independence Educational Publishers, Cambridge.

Dormor, D.J. (1992) *The Relationship Revolution: Cohabitation, Marriage and Divorce in Contemporary Europe*. One Plus One, London (for address, see below).

Dryden, C. (1999) *Being Married, Doing Gender*. Routledge, London.

Giddens, A. (1992) *The Transformation of Intimacy*. Polity, Cambridge.

Haskey, J. and Kiernan, K. (1989) 'Cohabitation in Britain: Characteristics and estimated numbers of cohabiting partners', *Population Trends*, vol. 58, pp.23–32.

Kiernan, K. and Estaugh, V. (1993) *Cohabitation: Extra–marital Childbearing and Social Policy*. Family Policy Studies Centre, London, Occasional Paper, No. 17 (for address, see below).

Rodgers, B. and Pryor, J. (1998) *Divorce and Separation: The Outcomes for Children*. The Joseph Rowntree Foundation, York (for address, see below).

Smart, C. (1984) *The Ties that Bind: Law, Marriage and the Reproduction of Patriarchal Relations*. Routledge and Kegan Paul, London.

Smart, C. and Neale, B. (1999) *Family Fragments?* Polity, Cambridge.

PARENTS AND CHILDREN

Backett, K. (1982) *Mothers and Fathers: A Study of the Development and Negotiation of Parental Behaviour*. Macmillan, Basingstoke.

Bainham, A., Day Sclater, S. and Richards, M. (eds) (1999) *What is a Parent? A Socio–Legal Analysis*. Hart, Oxford.

Boulton, M. (1983) *On Being a Mother: A Study of Women with Pre–School Children*. Tavistock, London.

Brannen, J. and O'Brien, M. (eds) (1996) *Children in Families: Research and Policy*. Falmer, London.

Department of Health (1989) *An Introduction to the Children Act 1989*, HMSO, London (for address, see below).

Donnellan, C. (ed.) (1995) *Lone Parents: Issues for the Nineties*. Independence Educational Publishers, Cambridge.

Donnellan, C. (ed.) (1996) *What are Children's Rights?* Independence Educational Publishers, Cambridge.

James, A. and Prout, A. (eds) (1990) *Constructing and Reconstructing Childhood.* Falmer, Basingstoke.

James, A., Jenks, C. and Prout, A. (1998) *Theorising Childhood.* Polity, Cambridge.

Lewis, C. and O'Brien, M. (eds) (1987) *Reassessing Fatherhood: New Observations on Fathers and the Modern Family.* Sage, London.

McKee, L. and O'Brien, M. (eds) (1982) *The Father Figure.* Tavistock, London.

Morrow, G. (1998) *Understanding Families: Children's Perspectives*, National Children's Bureau/Joseph Rowntree Foundation (for address, see below).

Qvortrup, J. *et al* (eds) (1994) *Childhood Matters: Social Theory, Practices and Politics.* Avebury, Aldershot.

FAMILY PROBLEMS

Dallos, R. and McLaughlin, E. (eds) *Social Problems and the Family.* Sage, London.

Dobash, R.E. and Dobash, R.P. (1992) *Women, Violence and Social Change.* Routledge, London.

Dobash, R.E. and Dobash, R.P. (eds) (1998) *Rethinking Violence Against Women.* Sage, London.

Donnellan, C. (ed.) (1995) *Violence in the Family: Issues for the Nineties.* Independence Educational Publishers, Cambridge.

Gelles, R.J. (1997) *Intimate Violence in Families.* Sage, London.

Hester, M., Kelly, L. and Radford, J. (eds) (1996) *Women, Violence and Male Power.* Open University Press, Buckingham.

Kitzinger, J. (1988) 'Defending Innocence: Ideologies of Childhood', *Feminist Review*, no. 28, pp.77–87.

Mullender, A. and Morley, R. (eds) (1994) *Children Living with Domestic Violence.* Whiting and Birch, London.

Pahl, J. (ed.) (1985) *Private Violence and Public Policy.* Routledge and Kegan Paul, London.

Stainton Rogers, W., Hevey, D. and Ash, A. (eds) (1989) *Child Abuse and Neglect: Facing the Challenge.* Batsford, London.

Yllo, K. and Bograd, M. (eds) (1988) *Feminist Perspectives on Wife Abuse.* Sage, London.

FAMILIES AND THE STATE

Donzelot, J. (1980) *the Policing of Families.* Huchison, London.

Fox, Harding, L. (1996) *Family, State and Social Policy.* Macmillan, Basingstoke.

Lasch, C. (1977) *Haven in a Heartless World*. Basic Books, New York.

Mount, F. (1982) *The Subversive Family*. Cape, London.

Parton, N. (1991) *Governing the Family: Child Care, Child Protection and the State*. Macmillan, Basingstoke.

Rodger, J.J. (1996) *Family Life and Social Control*. Macmillan, Basingstoke.

OTHER RESOURCES

Family Policy Studies Centre
Factsheet 3: One–Parent Families (undated).
Family Report 1: Families and the Law (1994).
Family Report 2: Children in Britain (1995).
Family Report 3: Families in Britain (1995).
Conference Report: Families and Parenting (1995).
Seminar Proceedings: Policies for Families: work, poverty and resources (1994).

Contact the *Family Policy Studies Centre* for a full list of their publications:
FPSC
9 Tavistock Place
London WC1H 9SN
Tel: 020 7388 5900
Email: fpsc@mailbox.ulcc.ac.uk
www.fpsc.org.uk

Other useful addresses and websites:
National Council for Family Proceedings
University of Bristol
Wills Memorial Building
Queens Road, Cllifton
Bristol BS8 1RJ
Tel: 0117 954 5381
email: n-c-f-p@bristol.ac.uk

The Children's Society
Edward Rudolph House
Margery Street
London WC1X 0JL
Tel: 020 7841 4400

One Plus One
Marriage and Partnership Research
14 Theobald's Road
London WC1X 8PF
Tel: 020 7831 5261
www.oneplusone.org.uk

The Joseph Rowntree Foundation funds research into various aspects of family life and publishes regular bulletings of the findings. Look up their Website at http://www.jrf.org.uk

Office Government publications can be obtained from:
The Stationery Office Ltd.
National Publishing
51 Nine Elms Road
London SW8 5DR
Tel: 020 7873 001

The Supporting Families Consultation Paper can be obtained from the Stationery Office (above) or accessed on the Home Office Website http://www.homeoffice.gov.uk.

Women's Aid Federation for England
www.womensaid.org.uk

RELATE
www.relate.org.uk

Tavistock Marital Studies Centre
www.tmsi.org.uk

Children's Legal Centre
www.essex.ac.uk/clc/

Families Need Fathers is an organisation that provides information and advice to parents who are trying to maintain contact with their children after separation or divorce. Visit their website at www.fnf.org.uk.

INDEX